Praying the Way Jesus Prayed

Praying the Way Jesus Prayed

Breaking through the Barriers That Keep Us from Connecting with God

MARK LINK, SJ

LOYOLA PRESS.
A JESUIT MINISTRY

Chicago

LOYOLA PRESS.
A JESUIT MINISTRY

3441 N. Ashland Avenue
Chicago, Illinois 60657
(800) 621-1008
www.loyolapress.com

Some material in this book was published in *Experiencing Prayer: Three Settings* by Mark Link, SJ (Allen, Texas: Argus Communications, 1984).

Scripture quotations are from the *Good News Bible*, the Bible in Today's English Version: Copyright © American Bible Society, 1976, 1992. Reprinted with permission.

Scripture texts in this work identified as NAB are taken from the *New American Bible with Revised New Testament and Revised Psalms* © 1991, 1986, 1970 Confraternity of Christian Doctrine, Washington, D.C. and are used by permission of the copyright owner. All Rights Reserved. No part of the *New American Bible* may be reproduced in any form without permission in writing from the copyright owner.

Excerpts from the English translation of *The Sacramentary (Revised Edition): Volume One: Sundays and Solemnities* © 1998, International Committee on English in the Liturgy, Inc. All rights reserved.

Cover image: Veer
Cover and interior design by Judine O'Shea

Library of Congress Cataloging-in-Publication Data
Link, Mark J.
  Praying the way Jesus prayed : breaking through the barriers that keep us from connecting with God / Mark Link.
      p. cm.
  ISBN-13: 978-0-8294-2725-7
  ISBN-10: 0-8294-2725-2
  1. Prayer—Catholic Church. 2. Jesus Christ—Prayers. I. Title.
  BV210.3.L56 2008
  248.3'2—dc22

                                                        2008029779

Printed in the United States of America
08 09 10 11 12 13 Bang 10 9 8 7 6 5 4 3 2 1

Contents

Personal Setting

1   We Go Off Alone *3*

2   We Marvel, Explore, and Converse *23*

3   We Personalize *47*

Small Group Setting

4   We Share and Support. *73*

Communal (Liturgical) Setting

5   We Gather. *93*

6   We Listen *105*

7   We Break Bread and Go Forth *117*

8   We Break through the Barriers *135*

Bibliography. *147*

Personal Setting

CHAPTER I

We Go Off Alone

Very early the next morning . . .
Jesus got up and left the house. He went out
of town to a lonely place where he prayed.

Mark 1:35

Former White House aide Charles Colson was reading *Mere Christianity* by C. S. Lewis. Suddenly, he put the book down, turned to his wife, Patty, and said, "Honey, you believe in God, don't you?"

"You know I do," she said.

Pushing the point, he said, "But have you ever thought about it deeply? Like, who is God and why did he create us—things like that?" Patty's look was one of "pure bafflement."

Later, Colson wrote:

> In the ten years we'd been married, I real-
> ized, we'd never discussed God. We'd never
> gone deep down and shared the faith within

us. How much on the surface are even our
closest relationships! Adapted from *Born Again*

Tragically, what Colson said of his relationship with
Patty is often true of our relationship with Jesus.

Outwardly, we are committed to Jesus. We try
to attend church regularly, follow his teaching, and
even wear a crucifix around our neck. Deep down,
however, we don't really know Jesus. We only know
about him.

Why is this the case? Why don't we know him
in a deep down way? One reason is that we've never
learned to communicate with him in a deep down
personal way—a truly prayerful way.

Some time ago, a magazine asked its readers what
topic they would like to hear covered more often in
Sunday homilies. The topic that led all the rest by a
wide margin was prayer.

There is in people today a desire to learn more
about prayer. People want to learn how to connect
with Jesus in a prayerful way. They want to learn how
to build a personal relationship with him.

How Jesus Prayed

One of the best ways to begin is to go to the Gospels
themselves with the sole intention of seeing when and
how Jesus prayed. What you find may surprise you; at

least it surprised me the first time I made a list of the places where Jesus prayed and how he prayed. My first surprise was to learn how *often* Jesus prayed.

Let me list just a few examples for you from the Gospel according to Luke.

After being baptized, Jesus prayed. Luke 3:21 After preaching and healing people, Jesus prayed. Luke 5:16 Before choosing the twelve apostles, Jesus spent the night "praying to God." Luke 6:12 Before multiplying the loaves and fishes, Jesus prayed. Luke 9:16 Before being transfigured on the mountain in the presence of Peter, James, and John, Jesus was praying. Luke 9:29 Before the disciples asked Jesus to teach them to pray, Luke says, "Jesus was praying." Luke 11:1

I'm just halfway through the Gospel, but you can already see how often Jesus prayed.

A second point that emerged in my study of the prayer of Jesus was this: Jesus not only prayed often, he often prayed by himself. That is, he went off all alone by himself to pray in solitude. For example, Mark tells us that Jesus "went out of town to a lonely place where he prayed." Mark 1:35 And Luke tells us that Jesus, "went up a hill to pray and spent the whole night there praying to God." Luke 6:12

Before developing the point that Jesus often prayed in solitude, let me clarify something. A story will help me make the point.

Henry David Thoreau was a philosopher, writer, and contemporary of Abraham Lincoln. Thoreau built a small cabin on the shores of Walden Pond, a secluded wilderness spot in Massachusetts. For two years, he lived there in solitude as an experiment in living.

Thoreau wrote a book, titled *Walden*, about his experiment. The sixth chapter of the book contains an interesting observation. Thoreau writes: "I had three chairs in my house; one for solitude, two for friendship, three for society."

Different Prayer Settings

Thoreau's statement contains a really important insight. Our human personality is made up of three dimensions: the personal (solitude), the interpersonal (friendship), and the communal (society).

Our psychological wholeness as persons depends on how well we attend to each of these three dimensions of our personality. If we respect the needs of each dimension, we grow as persons. If we do not, our growth suffers.

There are times when we need to be alone. There are times when we need the company of our family or a few close friends. Finally, there are times when we need to identify with and have the support of a larger community.

What is true of our psychological lives is also true of our spiritual lives. In other words, our prayer lives should also include three settings: personal ones, when we pray alone; small group settings, when we pray with family or friends; and communal settings, when we pray with the larger community.

The Gospels show that Jesus prayed in each of these three settings. First, there were times when Jesus went off and prayed alone. Second, there were times when Jesus prayed with family and friends. It was customary for Jewish families to pray together on a daily basis.

We also know from the Gospels that there were times when Jesus prayed together with close friends. Luke says, "Jesus took Peter, John, and James with him and went up a hill to pray." Luke 9:28

Third, Jesus also prayed with the community. Luke writes, "on the Sabbath [Jesus] went as usual to the synagogue." Luke 4:16 The third setting in which Jesus prayed was the communal one, or what today we often call the liturgical setting.

Personal Setting

The first prayer setting is personal. Jesus not only prayed in private himself, he also instructed his followers to do so. One day, Jesus said to his disciples, "But when you pray, go to your room, close the door, and pray to your Father." Matthew 6:6

One of my early heroes was Dorothy Day. She worked among the poor in New York City. Together with Peter Maurin, she founded the Catholic Worker Movement. When she died in 1980, the *New York Times* did not hesitate to call her "the most influential person in the history of American Catholicism."

Each day, Dorothy Day used to pray in private in a small, deserted neighborhood church. When her work made this impossible, she prayed whenever she found time and wherever she found herself—on a bus, walking down the street, or waiting for an appointment.

Like Dorothy Day, we all have periods of waiting each day. These waiting periods are opportunities for privacy and prayer. They are opportunities for touching base with ourselves and listening to inner voices that we never knew existed until we started listening to them.

Inner Seeing

The writer John Kord Lagemann tells an interesting story about himself. Early in his career, he faced a big decision. It involved changing jobs and moving his family to a different city. At the time, he was frantically trying to complete a manuscript that refused to hang together.

One day he threw down his pencil in disgust and decided to go downtown and to accept the new job.

On his way, he passed a barber shop. He decided to get his hair cut. That simple decision changed the whole course of his life. He writes:

> By the time I got up from the barber's chair I was at peace with myself and the world and sure of what to do. I turned down the job—a move I've never regretted—went home and finished my manuscript in five hours.

Later he asked himself: "What happened to me in that barber chair?"

Then it hit him. The waiting time in the chair had served a valuable purpose. It allowed his mind to clear up sufficiently so that he could see things clearly for the first time in weeks.

Let me underscore his point with a personal example. As a nineteen-year-old during World War II, I was stationed on the island of Saipan in the South Pacific. During our times off, several of us used to go for swims in a secluded spot just off the rocky cliffs of the island. It was a lovely place, completely surrounded by immense rocks.

When we arrived there, the waters were so clear that you could see fish swimming about and even the ripples in the sand ten feet below. After half an hour of threshing about in the pool, however, we stirred up the waters so much that you could no longer see the bottom or the fish.

Our minds are like the waters of that pool. They, too, get so clouded from the turmoil of daily living that we no longer see things clearly. We need to pause, as John Kord Lagemann did, to let the sand settle. A quiet, uninterrupted period does this.

Freedom

This brings us back to the kind of solitude and privacy Jesus had in mind when he said: "Go to your room, close the door, and pray to your Father." Matthew 6:6

Why did Jesus recommend that we find a place to pray that affords actual, physical solitude? Why did Jesus himself seek places of solitude in which to pray?

First, physical solitude allows us to pray in whatever way we want to. For example, if we feel like praying with outstretched arms, we are free to do so. If we feel like speaking to God out loud, we are free to do so. If we feel like singing or crying, we can do so without embarrassment.

Presence of God

Second and more important, actual physical solitude helps us to become more aware of the presence of God. An awareness of God's presence is the starting point of all serious prayer.

Awareness of God's presence means that we realize he is present to us, just as we are present to ourselves. In fact, he is more present to us than our own breath. Sometimes God makes his presence felt during times of prayer in a special way. If this happens, we simply rest in his presence.

I remember one of my students who found it difficult to rest in God's presence without speaking. One night he happened to be sitting on the rocky shore of Lake Michigan with his girl.

He said it was one of those really beautiful nights. They just sat there for a long time holding hands and saying nothing. They simply enjoyed being together listening to the water and watching it dance and sparkle in the moonlight.

That one experience helped him to appreciate how perfectly natural it is to rest in God's presence without speaking.

Feeling

This brings us to an important point about prayer that cannot be stressed enough: we should be careful not to equate feeling with praying. We humans are very emotional, and sometimes we let our emotions influence us more than they should.

In his book *The Taste of New Wine*, Keith Miller says that it used to bother him that he did not always feel God's presence during times of prayer. Then one day a friend explained to him that feeling was not the point of prayer. This insight gave Keith a new understanding of himself.

He said it suddenly occurred to him that he had been a kind of spiritual sensualist. He was always trying to feel God's presence at prayer. When he didn't feel it, he became depressed. He thought there was something wrong with the way he was praying. After Keith accepted his friend's insight, he began to pray without concern for whether he felt spiritual or not. For the first time in his life, he found that he could pray on raw faith. He writes:

> I found that the very act of praying this way later brings a closer sense of God's presence. And I realized a strange thing: that if a person in his praying has the *feeling*, he doesn't need the *faith*.
>
> I began to feel very tender toward God on those mornings during which I would pray without any conscious sense of his presence. I felt this way because at last I was giving back to him the gift of faith.

If God gives us a special awareness of his presence during prayer, fine. Any special effort on our part to make ourselves feel the presence of God, however, is nearly always wrong. An awareness of God's presence cannot be wished or willed into being. It is strictly a gift—a gift that God will give us from time to time.

Body Prayer

This brings up a third point about the prayer of Jesus. Jesus not only prayed often and alone, but he also prayed with his whole body. The great Egyptian leader Anwar Sadat had a very noticeable mark on his forehead from touching the ground so often as he bowed low in prayer. Praying with the *whole body* goes all the way back to early biblical times. Take, for example, this episode in the book of Exodus.

Joshua and his army were engaging the Amalekites in battle. Meanwhile, Moses, Aaron, and Hur were praying for the successful outcome of the battle on a hilltop. The book of Exodus says:

> As long as Moses held up his arms, the Israelites won, but when he put his arms down, the Amalekites started winning. When Moses' arms grew tired, Aaron and Hur brought a stone for him to sit on, while they stood beside him and held up his arms, holding them steady until the sun went down. In this way Joshua totally defeated the Amalekites. Exodus 17:11–13

There's also the example of Solomon. Recall how he prayed at the dedication of the temple. The first book of Kings says:

> Solomon went and stood in front of the altar, where he raised his arms and prayed, "Lord God of Israel, . . . Not even all of heaven is large enough to hold you, so how can this Temple that I have built be large enough? . . . Hear my prayers and the prayers of your people when they face this place and pray." I Kings 8:22–23, 27, 30

Finally, there is the example of Daniel. He used to pray in an upstairs room of his house where the windows faced Jerusalem. "There, . . . he knelt down at the open windows and prayed to God three times a day." Daniel 6:10

Praying with upraised hands, kneeling, or facing a certain direction are just a few examples of praying with the whole body found in the Bible.

Face Down

Jesus also involved his whole body in prayer. One way he did this is described by Luke when he writes that in the garden, "[Jesus] went off from [his disciples] about the distance of a stone's throw and knelt down and prayed." Luke 22:41

As the intensity of Jesus' agony mounted, Matthew says, "[Jesus] went a little farther on, threw himself face downward on the ground, and prayed." Matthew 26:39

Why did Jesus involve his body in prayer by kneeling and lying face down? Jesus understood that we are integral beings. Our bodies are a part of us, just as much as our minds and our hearts. The body, the mind, and the heart interact and affect one another.

Someone once said, "I kneel when I pray *not* because I feel reverent, but that I may *become* reverent." In other words, the mind not only affects the body, the body also affects the mind. In my own daily prayer I give great attention to the body.

For example, in private I frequently pray with my shoes off. Besides being comfortable, doing so reminds me of God's presence. God told Moses at the burning bush, "Take off your sandals, because you are standing on holy ground." Exodus 3:5 In my younger years, I also prayed seated on the floor with my legs crossed and with my lower back resting firmly against something.

The impact of the body on prayer, I have found from personal experience, is significant.

Eyes Raised

A second way that Jesus involved his body in prayer was that he used his eyes. For example, when he cured the deaf mute, Mark says, "Jesus looked up to heaven." Mark 7:34 While praying over the loaves and fishes, Jesus "looked up to heaven." Matthew 14:19 Finally, at the Last Supper when Jesus prayed to his Father for his disciples, Jesus "looked up to heaven." John 17:1

Some people find that closing their eyes helps them pray. Others find that letting them fall unfocused on the floor helps; this is how Zen monks fix their eyes in prayer. Still others find that fixing their eyes on a flickering candle, a picture, or some other object helps them to pray better.

There's an interesting story told by astronaut Ed White in *The Guideposts Treasury of Faith*. Ed, along with astronaut Jim McDivitt, made the Gemini 4 flight into space. When the two men arrived at Launch Pad 19 on June 3, 1965, they were both carrying medals given to them by Pope John XXIII. Ed had sewn his medal into the left leg of his space suit. Jim, on the other hand, hung his medal on the instrument panel of the spaceship. White wrote about it this way:

> Once we were in orbit and weightless, Jim's
> medal floated lazily on the end of its short

chain, reminding us constantly not only of the prayer Pope John had said for the astronauts but of the prayers of fellow Americans.

It's hard to describe the feeling that comes with the knowledge that 190 million people are praying for you. You have the sensation of not being yourself at all. It makes you feel very small and humble.

There are many ways to use your eyes in prayer. There's no set rule. When I pray, I do different things with my eyes depending on such things as my mood, the place where I am praying, and the time of day or night I am praying. Sometimes I close them. Sometimes I fix them on some object such as a crucifix. Sometimes I look up to heaven as Jesus did.

Praying Out Loud

A final way Jesus involved his body in prayer was by praying out loud. For example, when he healed the man who could not speak or hear, Jesus not only touched the man and raised his eyes to heaven but also "groaned" out loud, and said "'*Ephphatha*,' which means, 'Open up!'" Mark 7:34

Similarly, Jesus prayed out loud on the cross, "'Forgive them, Father! They don't know what they are doing.'" Luke 23:34 Just before Jesus died, he "cried out in a loud voice, 'Father! In your hands I place my spirit!'" Luke 23:46

Heightens Involvement

I'll never forget a conversation I had with one of my students. He came to my office one morning all excited about a "breakthrough" in prayer. He said, "Last night I was all alone at home. After finishing my homework, I decided to say my night prayers out loud. Wow! It really freaked me out. It made me conscious that I was really speaking to 'someone.'"

There's a delightful story about President Lyndon Johnson that underscores the idea of speaking to "someone." One morning he sat down to breakfast with his press secretary, Bill Moyers. The president bowed his head reverently and said, "Bill, will you say grace?"

Moyers began to pray in his trademark soft voice. He hadn't prayed one sentence before Johnson spoke up, saying, "Louder, Bill, I can't hear you!" Moyers didn't raise his head. He merely said, "Mr. President, I am not speaking to *you*." Then he went on with his prayer—speaking directly to God.

Personally, I find praying out loud especially helpful when I am tired or distracted. On these occasions, I often fall back on praying the Lord's Prayer out loud. I simply recite the Lord's Prayer a sentence at a time. After saying it, I pause briefly to reflect on its meaning. In this way I go through the entire prayer. When I finish the prayer, I repeat the process. At other times, I simply repeat a single word or phrase, like "Our Father." I let it echo in my heart. When the echo dies out, I merely repeat the word again.

Review

Let's now summarize what we have seen thus far concerning the way Jesus prayed.

First, we saw that Jesus prayed often. For example, he prayed at his baptism, during his ministry, before choosing his twelve disciples, before multiplying the loaves and fishes, before asking his disciples "Who do you say I am," at the time of his transfiguration, and before teaching his disciples to pray.

Second, we saw that Jesus prayed in three different settings. He prayed alone in solitude. He prayed with family and friends in small groups. He prayed with the larger community in the synagogue on the Sabbath.

Third, we saw that Jesus prayed with his body as well as with his mind and his heart. On some occasions, he knelt down. On other occasions, he looked up to heaven. And on still other occasions, he prayed out loud.

In our next chapter, we will complete our study of how Jesus prayed in solitude. Then, in subsequent chapters, we'll discuss prayer in small groups and with the larger community.

Prayer Model

Let me conclude with a story that summarizes and illustrates several of the points I have tried to make. The story comes from a book entitled *Down These Mean Streets* by Piri Thomas. Piri was a drug addict, an attempted killer, and a convict. His turf was Spanish Harlem in New York City.

Piri's life made a 180-degree turnaround one night in prison. He was lying on his cell bunk when it suddenly occurred to him what a tragic mess he had made of things. He felt an overwhelming need to pray.

He was sharing his cell with someone he called "the thin kid." He decided to wait until the kid was asleep before beginning his prayer. Thus a few minutes later, he climbed down from the top bunk and knelt on the cold floor. He wrote later:

> I couldn't play it cheap. I knelt at the foot of the bed and made like God was there in the flesh with me. I talked to him plain, no big words. I felt like I could even cry if I wanted

to, something I hadn't been able to do for years.

After Piri finished his prayer, a small voice said, "Amen." It was the thin kid. Piri writes:

> There we were, he, lying down, head on bended elbows, and I still on my knees. No one spoke for a long while. Then the kid whispered. "I believe in *Dios* also. Maybe you don't believe it, but I used to go to church, and I had the hand of God upon me. I felt always like you, and I feel now, warm, quiet, peaceful, like there's no suffering in our hearts."

After talking with the kid for a while, Piri climbed back into his bunk. "Good night, Chico," he said. "I'm thinking that God is always with us—it's just that we aren't with him."

Piri fell asleep thinking that he heard the kid crying softly. "Cry kid," he said to himself. "I hear even Christ cried."

Points to Ponder and Discuss

1. How typical do I think the relationship that Colson had with his wife, Patty, is when it comes to talking about prayer, God, and faith?

2. If someone found my wallet or my purse, what are some things in it that indicate I am a Christian?

3. Thoreau wrote in *Walden*: "I had three chairs in my house; one for solitude, two for friendship, three for society." What insight is contained in his statement?

4. We all have periods of waiting in our lives: walking down a street, driving to work, waiting for an appointment. To what extent do I use these as opportunities to pray and reflect?

5. The author says, "In private I frequently pray with my shoes off. Besides being comfortable, doing so reminds me of God's presence." What are some things that have helped me to pray better?

6. What posture do I find most helpful in praying? Where, when, how often, and how long do I pray?

7. Why did Jesus involve his body in prayer, just as he did his mind and his heart? How do I handle distractions and fatigue in prayer?

CHAPTER 2

We Marvel, Explore, and Converse

I know a Christian man who fourteen years ago
was snatched up to the highest heaven . . .
and there he heard things that cannot be put
in words.

2 Corinthians 12:2,4

Thomas Merton was one of the most influential religious writers of our time. He grew up without religion. At sixteen, he was orphaned. At twenty-three, he found Christ. At twenty-four, he became a Catholic. Two years later, he put everything he owned in a duffel bag, went down to Gethsemane, Kentucky, and became a Trappist monk.

He describes his faith journey in his autobiography, *The Seven Storey Mountain*. A milestone occurred in his teens. After graduating from high school, he toured Europe on his own.

Greatly moved by Europe's cathedrals, he started reading the Bible. One night something happened that would, eventually, change his whole life. He writes:

> I was in my room. It was night. The light was on. Suddenly . . . I was overwhelmed with a sudden and profound insight into the misery and corruption of my own soul. . . . I was filled with horror at what I saw. . . . And now I think for the first time in my life I really began to pray. . . . praying to the God I had never known, to reach down towards me out of his darkness and to help me to get free of the thousand terrible things that held my will in slavery.

Merton was still a long way from a full conversion, but he was now on track. Concerning this passage in Merton's autobiography Emilie Griffin writes in *Turning: Reflections on the Experience of Conversion*:

> So there came in Merton's life . . . a recognition of his own sinfulness and weakness, a growing hatred of his sins, and a growing will to be freed of them. But this took place over a period of time, with much indecision . . . and backsliding. Yet it seems that throughout it all Merton had the grace to pray.

Importance of Prayer

That is the key! The door to a new life is prayer. It is getting in touch—and staying in touch—with Jesus on a daily basis.

To illustrate the importance of daily prayer, Jamie Buckingham uses this example in his book *Power for Living*:

> I often drive from my home in Melbourne, Florida, on the east coast, to the central Florida city of Orlando—about seventy miles away. . . . We have an excellent Christian radio station in Melbourne, and I enjoy listening to music on my car radio. However, as I drive away from Melbourne I begin to lose the station on my radio. The station back in Melbourne is still broadcasting. My radio is still working. The trouble is I have moved too far away to get clear reception.

This simple example illustrates why daily prayer is so important. It keeps us in range of Jesus' voice. Only by keeping within range of his voice can we hear him knocking at the door of our heart and inviting us to a deeper relationship with him. Revelation 3:20

Critical Moment of Prayer

Spiritual writers agree that the critical moment in daily prayer is the first minute: placing ourselves in God's presence. It sets the mood and the spirit for the entire meditation.

In his book *How to Pray*, Fr. Bernard Basset, SJ, spells out the critical moment this way: "I must stop thinking of everything while I put myself in the presence of God: becoming aware that he is here in the room with me."

Joggers begin each daily physical exercise in a set way: stretching and preparing mentally for their run. So, too, prayers begin each daily "spiritual exercise" in a set way. One set way is to say the following prayer slowly and from the heart:

Father, you created me
and put me on earth for a purpose.
Jesus, you died for me
and called me to complete your work.
Holy Spirit, you help me carry out the work
for which I was created and called.
In your presence and name, Father,
Son, and Holy Spirit, I begin my meditation.
May all my thoughts and inspirations
have their origin in you and
be directed to your greater honor and glory.

The awareness of God's presence is a gift. If God gives it to me—as he does from time to time—then I simply remain quietly in his presence. Any effort on my part to make myself feel God's presence, however, is almost always wrong. To repeat: an awareness of God's presence is a gift.

Inner Dimension of Prayer

If you're a tennis player, you may have read *The Inner Game of Tennis* by W. Timothy Gallwey. In it he points out that when we watch a game of tennis, we see only the outer game. We see only the serves, moves, and volleys of the players.

What we don't see is the inner game—what is going on in the minds of the players. It is this invisible game that Gallwey writes about.

What is true of tennis is also true of prayer. It has an outer dimension and an inner dimension. The outer dimension or prayer is what we see: a person sitting in a chair, Bible or meditation book on the lap, and eyes closed. What we don't see is the inner dimension of prayer—that is, what is going on in the mind and the heart of the person.

In the first chapter, we explored the outer dimension. We used Jesus as our model. In this chapter, we will explore the inner dimension of prayer. Again, we will use Jesus as our model.

Three Prayer Forms

One way to approach the inner dimension of prayer is to do so in terms of three traditional prayer forms: contemplation, meditation, and conversation.

Often these three forms occur intertwined in the same prayer, like strands of wire in the same cable. It is hard to tell where one leaves off and another begins. An example will help to illustrate what we mean by each of these forms.

One of my students described a memorable prayer experience that had a deep impact on him. He said:

> One day after a game in a park, I went to a nearby fountain for some water. As I drank, I felt refreshment enter my tired body. Then I stretched out on the grass and looked up at the clouds in the sky. It was like I had never seen them before. I couldn't take my eyes off them [contemplation].
>
> After a while, I began to think: We need water for refreshment and strength, but where does water come from? Clouds, I thought. But where do clouds come from? Vaporized air. This thinking process went on until I got no answer. Or rather, I was left with only one answer: God [meditation].

For the next couple of minutes I just lay on the grass looking at the sky, marveling at what God must be like [contemplation]. Then I talked to God in my own words for a few minutes and started for home [conversation].

Contemplation

Contemplation is "seeing" persons, situations, events, and creation in a way in which we've never taken the time to see them before. Ultimately, it is seeing them as images of God and God's love for us.

It is clear from the preaching of Jesus that he was deeply contemplative. He spoke of the lilies of the field, the birds of the air, the sower in the field, the shepherd carrying home a stray sheep, and the fishermen casting their nets.

These were everyday scenes that everyone saw, but Jesus saw beyond them to something much more. He saw in them the image of his Father and the image of his Father's love for us.

Commenting on contemplation, Fr. Andrew M. Greeley says, "Contemplation is a casualty of the American way of life. We simply do not have time for it. We read poetry as we would a detective story.

We visit art museums as we would tour the Grand Canyon."

An excellent example of what he is talking about is a scene in the Broadway play *The Rainmaker* by Richard Nash. There is a dreamer in the play named Starbuck. But his dreams never come to pass.

One day he asks his friend, Lizzie, why his everyday world falls so short of his dream world. Lizzie says:

> I don't know. Maybe it's because you don't take time to see it. Always on the go—here, there, nowhere. Running away keeping your own company. Maybe if you'd keep company with the world . . .

Starbuck says doubtfully, "I'd learn to love it?" Lizzie responds:

> You might—if you saw it real. Some nights I'm in the kitchen washing the dishes. And Pop's playing poker with the boys. Well, I'll watch him real close. And at first I'll just see an ordinary middle-aged man—not very interesting to look at.
>
> And then, minute by minute, I'll see little things I never saw in him before. Good things and bad things—queer little habits I

> never noticed he had, and ways of talking I
> never paid any mind to.
>
> And suddenly I know who he is—and I
> love him so much I could cry! And I want to
> thank God I took the time to see him real.

That's what contemplation is all about. It's taking the time to see things as they really are. It's taking the time to see them real—as Jesus saw them.

I'll never forget a directed retreat I gave to some students several years ago in Chicago. One young man in particular made an outstanding retreat.

After it was over he said, "Well, Father, now it's back to reality!" I said, "Oh no, Mike, not back to reality! Back to unreality! The real world is not the one you're going back to. It's the one you have been in touch with on this retreat."

A year later, Mike came up to me and said, "Father, here's a copy of my term paper for English. You'll be especially interested in one part of it." Later on I read the paper. There on page five was what Mike wanted me to read. It was a reference to my remark to him after the retreat: about the real world, the spiritual world of faith and God. It had moved Mike deeply.

Prayer, especially contemplation, is the way we access and connect with this "real" world. Again, an example will illustrate this point.

Take the air space in which we live and move. It is saturated with trillions and trillions of electronic signals from cell phones, computers, radios, and television. These signals range from vivid color, to beautiful music, to human voices, to oceans of print.

We can't see, hear, or read these signals. We can't access them with our senses. The only way we can access them is by our cell phone, computer, radio, or television set.

It's the same with the spiritual world of faith and God. It surrounds us. Just as we need an electronic receiver to access the electronic world, so we need prayer, especially contemplation, to access the spiritual world of faith and God.

In other words, prayer, especially contemplation, is the way we get in touch with ultimate reality: the spiritual world of faith and God.

Meditation

The second prayer form is meditation. Scripture scholar William Barclay says in his book *The Gospel of Luke*:

> Many people saw steam raise the lid of a kettle; only James Watt went on to think of a steam engine. Many people saw an apple fall; only Isaac Newton went on to think out the law of gravity.

I would like to add that many people saw a shepherd return home with a lost sheep draped over his shoulders, but only Jesus went on to think of his Father's compassion for sinners. In a similar way, many people saw the lilies of the field and the birds of the air, but only Jesus went on to think of his Father's providence. And many people saw clouds come up in the western sky, but only Jesus went on to think of the coming of his Father's kingdom.

Meditation is thinking about something. It is asking, "What might this experience, this situation, or this event be saying to us?" To put it more directly, what might God be saying to us through this experience, this situation, or this event?

If contemplation helps us to see the created world as it really is—the work of God—meditation helps us access what God is saying to us through the things he has made. Thus, St. Paul says:

> Ever since the world began, God's invisible attributes, this is to say his everlasting power and deity, have been visible to the eye of reason, in the things he has made." Romans 1:20
> New English Bible (NEB)

A true story from *Putting Forgiveness into Practice* by Doris Donnelly shows how God can speak to us, not only through the things he has made but also through the events and situations of everyday life.

A seven-year-old boy was riding with his two brothers. They were acting up in the backseat of the family car. The boys' mother was driving. She had just gone through a painful divorce from a faithless husband who had deserted his family.

Suddenly, the mother spun around in the car and slapped the seven-year-old across the face. "You! The only reason I had you," she screamed, "was to keep your father. I never wanted you! I hate you!" That scene cut into the sensitive child's memory like a knife.

In the years that followed, his mother continued to resent him. The years passed. Then one day in his early twenties, the young man began thinking about the strained situation between his mother and himself. He decided do something about it. This is how he decided to go about it:

"I put myself in my mother's place. Here she was, a high school graduate with no money, no job, and a family of four to support" [contemplation].

Then, he began to think about how this must have affected his mother: "how powerless, lonely, hurt, and depressed she must have felt. I thought of the anger, the fear, the pain that must have been there. And I thought of how much I must have reminded her of the failure of her young hopes" [meditation].

Suddenly, he saw the situation in a new way: from his mother's point of view. Then, God's grace took over. He called her, and they set up a time to meet. He described what happened:

"I told her I understood and that I loved her." Then something beautiful happened. He said, "We wept in each other's arms for what seemed to be hours. It was the beginning of a new life for me, for us."

That touching story illustrates how contemplation helps us to see things in a new way. It also shows how meditation helps us take the second step and respond to the reality that we now see.

Conversation

The third form of prayer is often referred to as conversation prayer. It consists of speaking to God and listening when God speaks to us.

Some years ago, Fr. Stephen Doyle, OFM, penned this imaginative dialogue in *Hi Time*, a publication for young people. It went like this:

"Charlie, how is your wife?" "She's fine, I think." "You think? Don't you know?" "Well, she and I aren't talking." "Have you two had a fight? Aren't you getting along?" "Oh, no, everything is fine; we just don't talk to each other." "How can things be fine, if you don't

even communicate?" "Really, everything is
just perfect; we just don't feel the need to talk
to each other."

If you overheard that conversation, you couldn't help
but suspect that Charlie's marriage was in serious
trouble. When communication deteriorates, so does
the relationship. This is true, also, of our relationship
with God. Communication is a gauge of our nearness
to or distance from another.

Speaking to God normally takes one of two forms:
using traditional prayers (fixed prayers) or spontaneous prayers (free prayers).

Traditional Prayers

One Sunday afternoon, Derrell Doré and eleven other
men were on a drilling rig in the Gulf of Mexico. The
steel platform on which the rig was located was about
half the size of a football field. It was being towed
to a new location. Suddenly, it began to tip badly to
one side. Mountainous waves and a strong wind were
throwing it off balance.

Seconds later, it went crashing into the sea, capsiz-
ing the platform and pulling it down into the deep
waters. Doré was trapped inside a room in the platform. It quickly filled with water, except for a large air

pocket that attached itself to the ceiling. It was this air bubble that kept Doré from drowning.

Twenty-two hours later, a diver discovered Doré. Later that day in a hospital, Doré told his wife:

> I prayed words that I had prayed as a youngster, words that, until now, had no such intense meaning for me. . . . Again and again I said those words:
>
> "O my Jesus, forgive us our sins. Save us from the fires of hell and lead all souls to heaven, especially those who are most in need of thy mercy." "Trapped at the Bottom of the Sea" from *The Guideposts Treasury of Love*

That prayer is sometimes added to each decade of the rosary and is a good example of what we mean by a traditional or memorized prayer. The older I get, the more I find that in times of grave danger people turn to memorized prayers. Dr. Sheila Cassidy did it during her imprisonment in Chile. Author Joni Eareckson Tada did it after a diving accident in the Chesapeake Bay.

Examples like this could be multiplied. They all point to one thing: In times of danger and difficulty we instinctively turn to memorized prayers—

prayers that we have learned by heart and that come spontaneously from our heart.

Traditional Prayers and Jesus

The book of Psalms played a key role in the life and worship of God's people. It put into song and prayer the history, beliefs, and feelings of the people. More than any other book of the Bible it shows how Jews prayed to God in times of sadness and in times of joy.

Jesus grew up praying these psalms. Like most Jews, he committed many of them to memory. Besides praying the psalms in the synagogue service each Sabbath, Jews prayed them in their homes on a daily basis. Psalm 119:164 reads: "Seven times a day I praise you" (NAB).

The most memorable situation when we find Jesus praying the psalms is on the cross. In this critical moment of his life, he did what so many people do in similar moments. He turned to traditional prayers. Matthew's Gospel describes that moment this way:

> At noon the whole country was covered with darkness, which lasted for three hours. At about three o'clock Jesus cried out in a loud shout, *"Eli, Eli, lema sabachthani?"* which means, "My God, my God, why did you abandon me?" Matthew 27:45–46; Psalm 22:1

If you wanted to know what was going on in the mind and heart of Jesus as he hung in agony on the cross, you could do no better than to read Psalm 22. An excerpt from it reads:

> My God, my God,
> why have you abandoned me?
> I have cried desperately for help, . . .
> But I am no longer a human being;
> I am a worm, . . .
> They gamble for my clothes . . .
> O Lord, don't stay away from me!
> Come quickly to my rescue!"

Psalm 22:1, 6, 18, 19

Spontaneous Prayer

The second form that conversation prayer takes is spontaneous prayer.

One of my favorite examples of spontaneous prayer occurred at a critical moment in the Civil War just before the Battle of Gettysburg.

Lee's army was heading north, and Lincoln knew that a defeat on Northern soil would mean the loss of Washington. It also would mean that both England and France would probably join the Confederacy. President Abraham Lincoln told General Daniel Sickles:

I went to my room and got down on my knees.
Never had I prayed with so much earnestness.
I felt I must put all my trust in Almighty
God. He gave us the best country. He alone
could save it. I had tried my best to do my
duty and had found myself unequal to the
task. The burden was more than I could bear.
I asked God to help us and give us victory. I
was sure my prayer was answered. I had no
misgivings about the result at Gettysburg.

Lincoln Talks by Emmanuel Hertz, page 559

Spontaneous prayer has a long biblical history. An example is Jeremiah's famous prayer. In it he complains to God for calling him to be a prophet:

Lord, you deceived me . . .
you have overpowered me. . . .
I am ridiculed and scorned all the time
because I proclaim your message. . . .
Even my close friends wait for my downfall.
Curse the day I was born." Jeremiah 20:7, 8, 10, 14

Spontaneous prayer is speaking to God from the
heart. It is bringing God into every situation of my
life, when I am confused, when I am happy, when
I am hurting, when I need help or guidance, and

especially after falling into sin. Psalm 51 is a good example of this. Its Hebrew title reads "A psalm by David, after the prophet Nathan had spoken to him about his adultery with Bathsheba." It reads:

> O God, . . .
> I have sinned against you—
> Remove my sin, and I will be clean;
> > wash me, and I will be whiter than
> > snow. . . .
> Create a pure heart in me, O God,
> > and put a new and loyal spirit in me.
> Do not banish me from your presence;
> do not take your holy spirit away from me.
>
> Psalm 51:1, 4, 7, 10–11

Jesus also used spontaneous prayer. Luke 22:21–22 The most memorable moment when we find Jesus praying spontaneously is at the Last Supper. John describes that moment this way:

> Jesus . . . looked up to heaven and said, "Father, . . . I have made you known to those you gave me. . . . I kept them safe by the power of your name. . . . May they be in us, just as you are in me and I am in you."
>
> John 17:1, 6, 12, 21

Listening Prayer

One of my favorite stories about listening comes from the Depression years. Those were years when vast numbers of people were unemployed. A man saw an ad for a telegraph operator. He hurried to the address listed in the ad.

When he got there, the room was jammed with applicants. The man was crestfallen. As he stood there wondering what to do, he heard a steady flow of dots and dashes over the heavy drone of conversation. Suddenly, his eyes lit up. He dashed over to a door marked "Private," turned the doorknob, and went inside.

In a few minutes, he came out smiling. He had the job. The employer told the rest of the applicants that they could leave. Well, as you might imagine, there was an angry outcry from the group.

"We demand an explanation," someone shouted. "This young man comes in late, bucks the line, and you hire him." The employer paused a moment, and then said, "You have your explanation. All you have to do is listen to the dots and dashes."

Everyone stopped and listened. Over and over the dots and dashes repeated the same message it had been repeating for an hour: "If you hear this, come in, the job is yours. If you hear this, come in, the job is yours."

God often speaks to us. He speaks to us through Scripture, through other people, through events, and through our own inner faculties. Unfortunately, like the applicants in the room, we are too busy talking to others. We don't hear God. A passage where we find Jesus listening to his Father is found in John's Gospel. It begins with Jesus speaking:

> "Now my heart is troubled—and what shall I say? Shall I say, 'Father, do not let this hour come upon me'? But that is why I came—so that I might go through this hour of suffering. Father, bring glory to your name!"
>
> Then a voice spoke from heaven, "I have brought glory to it, and I will do so again."
> John 12: 27–28

Jesus heard the Father's voice. Others said, "it was thunder, while others said, 'An angel spoke to him!'"
John 12:29

So how and when should we listen during our own prayer conversations with God? One such occasion is reading Scripture. Commenting on how to listen to God's words, Armand Nigro, SJ, makes this recommendation:

> Pause between the phrases so that the echo and meaning of the words can sink into you slowly like soft rain into thirsty soil.

You may want to keep repeating a word or phrase. . . .

Praying with Scripture this way is an experience of listening to God. Do not try to make applications or search for profound meanings and implications or conclusions or resolutions. These usually "junk-up" our prayer. Be content to listen simply and openly as a child.

Commenting on how God speaks to us through people and events, Louis Evely writes in *Our Prayer*:

Even those who do not know God sometimes recognize God suddenly in the presence of a truly religious person, happening, or event. They are suddenly forced to say: "There is God. . . ."

God talks to us at a level in ourselves that we cannot reach . . . an inner dimension that we did not know we possessed until God declared himself in it.

St. Francis de Sales, one of the great spiritual guides of all time, sums up the topic of prayer this way: "The chief exercise of prayer is to speak to God and to hear God speak in the bottom of your heart."

Points to Ponder and Discuss

1. John Henry Cardinal Newman once said that there is no such thing as a sudden conversion. What *is* sudden is the realization that I went through a conversion process. How does Merton's story illustrate that?

2. Jamie Buckingham talks about keeping in range of God's voice. What does he mean?

3. How do I begin my prayer? Why is this a critical moment? Why do I think God gives us only an occasional awareness of his presence?

4. Have I ever had a prayer experience like the one the student had in the park after his game?

5. What does the author mean by the electronic world? The faith world? Explain the similarity between the ways we connect with each world.

6. St. Paul says that "both God's eternal power and his divine nature are perceived in the things he has made." How is this an example of how contemplation and meditation can work together?

7. Why do I think so many people turn to memorized prayer in time of danger or difficulty? Recall a time when I turned to prayer in one of these situations. What is my favorite prayer?

8. The author says that God speaks to us through Scripture, through other people, through events,

through our own inner faculties. Can I recall a time when God seemed to speak to me through one of these? What made me think God did speak to me?

CHAPTER 3

We Personalize

One day Jesus was praying in a certain place.
When he had finished, one of the disciples
said to him, "Lord, teach us to pray."

Luke 11:1

We may think of ourselves as being made up of four
levels. The first level is the *sense* (skin) level. At this
level, I can look at you and you can look at me, and
we can see how we differ from each other. At this
level, we collect data from the world around us and
store it in our mind.

The second level is the *conscious* (mind) level. At
this level, I know what's going on in my mind; you
know what is going on in yours; but we can only
guess what's going on in each other's. At this level,
we process in our minds the data we collect at the
sense level.

The third level is the *subconscious* (heart) level.
At this level, I don't know what's going on in my

subconscious; you don't know what's going on in yours; but it is affecting us both profoundly. This level is the one in which we experience movements of the spirit. For example, we say "That touched my heart" or "My heart is singing for joy."

The fourth level is the *sanctuary* (soul) level. St. Paul had this level in mind when he said, "your body is the temple of the Holy Spirit." 1 Corinthians 6:19 Jesus also had it in mind when he said, "the Kingdom of God is within you." Luke 17:21 At this level, the divine and the human meet and embrace.

Personality Types

The Myers-Briggs Type Indicator (MBTI) test has been designed to help us understand how the combined activity of these four levels (sense, conscious, subconscious, and sanctuary) impact and shape our personality.

At the risk of oversimplification, we may say there are four basic personality types: *realist, intellectual, free spirit,* and *idealist.* Here's a brief preview of them.

Realists tend to have a practical bent. They are the people to whom we turn to get things done. Into this category fall schoolteachers and public servants.

Intellectuals are among those we depend upon to advance our technical and human progress. Research scholars, physicists, and computer programmers fall into this category.

Next come the *free spirits*. They tend to have creative minds. They are the people who inject a little fun and relaxation into our lives. Among these are our entertainers.

Finally come the *idealists*. They are perfectionists. They keep us focused on the ideal. In this category we might put our environmentalists, our poets, and our contemplatives.

Personality and Prayer

One of the most popular and oldest methods of prayer is known by its Latin name: *lectio divina*. It may be translated as "sacred reading." There are slightly different versions or variations of it. We will follow four steps, known by the Latin names *lectio* (reading), *meditatio* (thinking), *oratio* (praying), and *contemplatio* (contemplation).

These four prayer forms come into play at each of the four levels of the human person as follows:

prayer form	personality level
lectio (reading)	sense (skin)
meditatio (thinking)	conscious (mind)
oratio (speaking)	subconscious (heart)
contemplatio (listening)	sanctuary (soul)

Realists: *Lectio*

Realists tend to relate better to the *reading* phase of prayer. They try to picture—or make real—for themselves the Bible passage they are reading.

For example, they put themselves in the shoes of one of Jesus' disciples and imagine what they saw, heard, and felt when Jesus did or said something.

Intellectuals: *Meditatio*

Intellectuals tend to relate better to the thinking phase of prayer. They ponder the passage for any deeper meaning it may contain. For example, they might ask themselves why Jesus did or said something precisely in that way.

Free Spirits: *Oratio*

Free spirits tend to relate better to the speaking phase of prayer. For example, they are quite comfortable speaking to Jesus from the heart about how they feel in response to something he said or did.

Idealists: *Contemplatio*

Finally, idealists tend to relate to the listening phase of prayer. For example, they may read through the biblical passage slowly, stopping periodically to listen in the depth of their being to what Jesus might wish to say to them.

Matching Personality and Prayer

Let's now take a more detailed look at each of these four personality profiles and the four prayer forms by which they tend to approach God.

Before beginning, we should mention two helpful books on this topic. The first is *Please Understand Me* by David Keirsey and Marilyn Bates. Interestingly, they note that roughly 40 percent of us are classified as realists and another 40 percent as free spirits. Roughly 10 percent are classified as intellectuals and another 10 percent as idealists. They also give detailed descriptions of each personality type.

The second book is *Prayer and Temperament* by Chester P. Michael and Marie C. Norrisey. They treat the topic in detail and select the following four saints as being representative of each of the four personality types:

Ignatius of Loyola	realist
Thomas Aquinas	intellectual
Francis of Assisi	free spirit
Augustine of Hippo	idealist

Finally, they give a helpful list of prayer suggestions to help us experience the spirituality of each. Detailed references and discussions of both of the above books are available on the Internet.

Ignatian Temperament

Ignatius of Loyola was born in Spain just before the discovery of America. His parents died before he was sixteen, and he went to live with a family friend.

He became skilled at horse riding and in the use of the sword, the dagger, and the crossbow. It is not too surprising then that he became a soldier. In combat his right leg was shattered by a cannonball. While recovering, he went through a conversion so dramatic that it changed the course of his life.

He went on to found the Society of Jesus (Jesuits) who currently operate universities and high schools in 112 different countries.

Ignatius is widely known for his book *The Spiritual Exercises of St. Ignatius*. Actually, it is more of a collection of orderly notes than a book. It is not for a person "making" the Spiritual Exercises, but for the director guiding the person through them.

Michael and Norrisey use an interesting example to characterize the temperament of realists like St. Ignatius, saying they have a "very strong sense of duty and obligation, whether it be to God or to fellow human beings." They are "usually the people who continue going to church even though religion loses its appeal for the other three temperaments."

They "want to be givers rather than receivers." They are down-to-earth, practical, disciplined, and highly focused, especially when it comes to areas of education, the common good, social justice, and leadership.

Nowhere is this "practical, disciplined, focused" mentality more clearly evident than in the "Principle and Foundation" of *The Spiritual Exercises of St. Ignatius*. A free translation of it reads:

> I believe that I was created to share my life and my love with God and other people, forever.
>
> I believe that God created all the other things to help me achieve this goal.
>
> I believe that I should use the other things that God created insofar as they help me attain my goal and abstain from them insofar as they hinder me.
>
> It follows that I should not prefer certain things to others. That is, I should not value, automatically, health over sickness, wealth over poverty, honor over dishonor, or a long life over a short one.
>
> I believe my sole norm for valuing and preferring a thing should be this: How well

does it help me attain the end for which I was created?

The spirit of the Ignatian temperament is spelled out even more concretely in the "Prayer for Generosity," attributed to Ignatius. It reads:

Lord, teach me to be generous.
Teach me to serve you as you deserve;
to give and not to count the cost;
to fight and not to heed the wounds;
to toil and not to seek for rest;
to labor and not to ask for reward;
except to know that I am doing your will.

Ignatian Prayer

The Ignatian approach to prayer is detailed in *The Spiritual Exercises*. To illustrate, take Ignatius's approach to the crucifixion of Jesus. Ignatius would have us go back in our imagination to Calvary and experience what John or Mary, the mother of Jesus, saw, felt, and heard. A creative treatment of this prayer approach is found in "The Traveller," a story in Richard Matheson's collection *Third from the Sun*.

The story goes something like this: A scientist, Professor Paul Jairus, is part of a research team that develops an energy screen that allows people to go back in time.

The first trip is scheduled to take off a few days before Christmas. Jairus is chosen to make the trip. He decides to go back to Calvary to witness the crucifixion of Jesus.

He is a nonbeliever and anticipates finding the facts very different from those in the Gospel narrative. When the moment comes for his journey back in time, he steps inside the energy screen.

The trip goes as planned, and the energy screen sets down on target. Calvary is filled with people. All eyes are focused on the three men fastened to crosses. Immediately, Jairus gets permission from the Command Center to move closer to the three victims. As he does, his eyes come to rest on Jesus. Suddenly, something unanticipated happens. Jairus feels drawn to Jesus as a tiny piece of metal is drawn to a powerful magnet. He is deeply moved by the love radiating from Jesus. It's something that he's never experienced in his life.

Then contrary to all of his expectations, the events unfold exactly as described in the Gospel. Jairus is visibly shaken. The Command Center senses that he is becoming emotionally involved and orders him to prepare for his immediate return to the twentieth century. Jairus protests, but to no avail.

The return trip goes smoothly. When Jairus steps from the energy screen, it is clear he is a changed man. Matheson ends his story with this comment: "It was Christmas Eve and it was a lovely time to find a faith."

The prayer approach of realists like Ignatius is to make the Gospel events come alive and become real. For example, you imagine yourself as someone like the centurion in charge of the crucifixion. You see, hear, and feel everything he saw, heard, and felt. Hopefully, you will make it so alive and real in your imagination that you will end up saying what the centurion said, "Truly this man was the Son of God!" Mark 15:39 NAB

Thomistic Temperament

Thomas Aquinas was one the bright lights of the thirteenth century. He was born into a prosperous family that had plans for him. He had his own plans, however, and applied for and was received into the Order of St. Dominic.

His two brothers retaliated, kidnapping him and confining him for nearly two years. During this period, every effort was made to destroy his vocation. When it was clear that nothing would change his mind, he was allowed to return to the order. He went on to become one of the outstanding, all-time theologians of the Church.

His theological method contrasted sharply with the methods of his time, which relied heavily on authority. His ruthless quest for the truth led him to do the unheard of: He integrated the insights of pagan philosophers like Aristotle into his works. The most celebrated of these works was the *Summa Theologica*, "a view of the whole" of theology.

Intellectuals like Thomas tend to be relentless when it comes to an intellectual challenge. Their approach is much like that of scientists in pursuit of a scientific mystery. They are driven in all they do, whether it be sports, business, science, or the spiritual life.

One of my favorite stories of someone who was driven in his search for truth is that of Siddhartha Gautama, a fifth-century BC prince in India who would become the Buddha. One version of his story goes something like this:

Siddhartha's family lived in a royal compound that shielded him from the many ugly sights that lay outside it. One day, he slipped outside the compound without his family noticing. He saw four sights that changed his life forever.

The first sight was a sick man who was coughing and spitting up blood. Suddenly, Siddhartha realized that one day his health would fade and he would be like the sick man. This disturbed him.

The second sight that Siddhartha saw was that of an old man. He had no teeth and could hardly see or walk. Again, it occurred to him that some day he would be old and feeble like this unfortunate man. This disturbed him deeply.

The third sight he saw was that of a dead man. This disturbed him even more than did the previous two sights. He realized that the life that pulsed vibrantly through his body would someday leave him and he would no longer exist. This disturbed him even more deeply.

The fourth sight Siddhartha saw was a holy man. This disturbed Siddhartha even more than all of the other sights put together. Why? The holy man was not, in the least, disturbed by any of the three previous sights. What did the holy man know that Siddhartha didn't know?

This set him on a quest to learn what the holy man knew. He left the royal compound, abandoned his life of comfort, fasted, and wandered alone through barren places seeking an answer; but no answer came.

Then one day in his wanderings, Siddhartha came to a Bodhi tree. He sat down in its shade and began a period of prolonged meditation. Hours stretched to days, days into weeks.

Then one day enlightenment came: "True happiness is not to be found in this world, but only in the world beyond."

Thomistic Prayer

The search for truth is a prime characteristic of the Thomistic temperament. This is reflected in intellectuals' approach to prayer. Questions like *what?*, *why?*, and *how?* are signposts on the path of their prayer. Their meditation might begin in order simply to understand why or how the cross, a cruel tool of torture, became the *sign* identifying Christians as followers and friends of Jesus.

Meditation shows the cross to be a dramatic sign. It says in a visible way what Jesus said in a verbal way: "The greatest love you can have for your friends is to give up your life for them." John 15:13

Further meditation shows that the cross is not just a sign. It is also a dramatic *invitation*. It says in a visible way what Jesus said in a verbal way: "Love one another, just as I love you." John 15:12

Finally, meditation shows that the cross is not just a sign and an invitation. It is also a *revelation*. It says in a visible way what Jesus said so often: Love entails suffering. Jesus put it this way: "If you want to come with me, you must forget yourself, take up your cross every day, and follow me. For if you want to save your own life, you will lose it, but if you lose your life for my sake, you will save it." Luke 9:23–24

In brief, the intellectual's approach to the crucifixion is to probe for its deeper meaning and apply it to our everyday lives. It is a sign of love, an invitation to love, and a revelation about love.

That brings us to St. Francis of Assisi and the free spirit's temperament and prayer approach.

Franciscan Temperament

St. Francis was born into a wealthy Italian family. As a teenager, he was a playboy and a spendthrift. He used his generous allowance to pay the bills of his rowdy friends.

In the year 1202, hostilities broke out between the towns of Assisi and Perugia. Young Francis joined the army of Assisi. During the conflict, he was captured and spent the next year of his life confined in a dirty, filthy dungeon.

After his release, it took him a full year to regain his broken health. One morning at Mass, the Gospel reading was Jesus' instruction to his disciples to preach the good news to the people in the surrounding villages. Jesus went on to tell them to take nothing with them, but to trust God completely for all their material needs. Luke 9:1–6

That Gospel passage changed St. Francis's life and gave it a whole new direction. His charismatic personality inspired other young people to join him; the Franciscan lifestyle was born. The rest is history.

Francis transferred his generous spirit to his relationship with Jesus. He fell in love with Jesus, embraced his invitation to love others as he loves us, picked up his cross, and followed him daily.

Michael and Norrisey describe the temperament of Francis and other free spirits as follows: Free and unconfined, they are "able to do whatever their inner spirit moves them to do." They tend to be "impulsive and dislike being tied down by rules." They are "cheerful, lighthearted, witty, charming." They are "good at unsnarling messes, and able to get things going." They make good troubleshooters, negotiators, and diplomats.

Franciscan Prayer

I once read that as Pope Pius XII lay dying, his final request was to listen to the third movement of Beethoven's Ninth Symphony.

I don't know about Pius XII's personality temperament, but that request was certainly free-spirited. It was an uninhibited way for a *pope* to raise his mind and heart to God at the most critical moment of his life. I found myself admiring him the more for it.

Another example of the free-spirited or Franciscan approach to prayer is the French scientist Louis Pasteur. One day an assistant entered his lab and found him bent over his microscope as if in prayer. Pasteur looked up and said, "Come in."

The assistant then noticed that Pasteur was looking at a leaf from a tree. He said, "I didn't want to disturb you. I thought you might be praying." Pasteur said, "I was."

How might a free spirit approach the crucifixion of Jesus? An example occurs in the novel *Legion* by William Peter Blatty.

In one scene, Jewish detective Lt. Kinderman is sitting all alone in a church. An elderly priest has been murdered while hearing confessions.

After a while, Kinderman lifts his eyes slowly to a large crucifix above the altar. As he gazes at the face of Jesus, his own face softens, and a quiet wonder comes to his eyes. He begins to speak to Jesus out loud. His monologue goes something like this:

> Who are you? God's son? No, you know I don't believe that. I just asked to be polite. I don't know who you are, but you are

Someone. Do you know how I know? From what you said.

When I read, "Love your enemy," I tingle. No one on earth could ever say what you said. No one could even make it up. Who could imagine it? The words knock you down. Who are you, and what do you want from us?

Kinderman's monologue is a beautiful example of how a free spirit might approach the crucifixion of Jesus. Free spirits simply follow the lead of the heart and respond to it in an uninhibited way. They might even end up singing, or dancing as David did before the Ark of the Covenant. 2 Samuel 6:14

Let's conclude the Franciscan approach to prayer with "The Peace Prayer" attributed to St. Francis:

Lord, make me an instrument of your peace;
where there is hatred, let me sow love;
where there is injury, pardon;
where there is doubt, faith;
where there is despair, hope;
where there is darkness, light;
where there is sadness, joy.
Grant that I may not so much
seek to be consoled as to console;
to be understood as to understand;

to be loved as to love;
for it is in giving that we receive;
it is in pardoning that we are pardoned;
and it is in dying that we are born to eternal life.

Augustinian Temperament

Augustine was born in Africa in the fourth century. His adolescence was a stormy period. In his twenties he became a professor of rhetoric in Milan, but his personal life remained as chaotic as ever. One day he broke into tears and cried out to God, "How long will you be angry with me? Forever? Why not at this very hour put an end to my evil life?" He was crying out like this when, suddenly, he heard what seemed to be the voice of a child, saying, "Take and read!" He writes in his *Confessions*:

> I stood up, got a Bible, and opened it. The first words my eyes fell upon were from Paul's letter to the Romans: "Throw off the works of darkness. . . . put on the Lord Jesus Christ, and make no provision for the desires of the flesh. Romans 13:12–14

When Augustine read this, he stopped. There was no need to go on. He was home. He writes: "My heart was suddenly flooded with a light that erased all my doubts."

Augustine and other idealists tend to be frank. They are skilled communicators, be it through the spoken word or through the written word.

High on their list of concerns both for themselves and others are authenticity, self-understanding, and self-improvement, especially in the area of spiritual growth and perfection. A goal for them in human growth and development is harmony between their inner self and their external life and activity.

Augustinian Prayer

Recall how the Ignatian and realist approach to prayer was to go back in their imagination to the original biblical event. The point was to make an event like the Crucifixion come alive and become real to the point that they would say with the centurion, "This man was really the Son of God!" Mark 15:39

The approach of the idealist is just the opposite.

Rather than go back in their imagination to the Crucifixion, idealists, like Augustine, would bring the event into the present. A good example of this prayer approach is Joni Eareckson Tada.

One afternoon in July, seventeen-year-old Joni Eareckson was totally paralyzed in a diving accident.

The beautiful girl who thrilled horse-show audiences with her riding skill was placed in a Stryker frame and rotated every thirty minutes—thirty minutes facing the ceiling; thirty minutes facing the floor—to keep her from getting body sores.

She went from 120 pounds to 80 pounds. Her skin turned yellow, and her teeth turned black from the medication she was given. In desperation for something to hold on to, she turned reluctantly to the Bible. A young man read it to her on a regular basis.

One day Joni and this young man were reading the book of Lamentations by the prophet Jeremiah. In the book, the battle-torn city of Jerusalem is addressed as a fallen woman. Jeremiah begins, saying of Jerusalem, "All night long she cries; tears run down her cheeks. Of all her former friends, not one is left to comfort her." Lamentations 1:2

Applying these sad words to her helpless situation, Joni writes, "Oh, God, how true. And I can't even wipe my own tears away!"

Jeremiah continues, "He sent fire from above, a fire that burned inside me. He set a trap for me and brought me to the ground." Lamentations 1:13 Joni writes: "The diving accident . . . my total paralysis . . ."

Jeremiah continues: "The Lord gave me to my foes, and I was helpless against them." Lamentations 1:14 Joni writes: "In bed for a year, completely dependent on orderlies and nurses."

Jeremiah continues, "He has left my flesh open and raw, and has broken my bones." Lamentations 3:4 Joni writes: "The bedsores, stitches, bone surgery." Then Joni writes:

> My studies in the Scriptures began in earnest now. I'd visualize Jesus standing beside my Stryker. . . . saying specifically to me, "Lo, I am with you always."

By this process of bringing the biblical event into the present, Joni writes, "I discovered that the Lord Jesus Christ could indeed empathize with my situation. On the cross . . . he was immobilized, helpless, paralyzed." *Joni: An Unforgettable Story* by Joni Eareckson Tada

Gradually, a great change took place in Joni. Though still paralyzed, she's become an acclaimed artist (she holds a pen in her teeth) and author of a best seller, played the lead in a movie of her life, and become a popular motivational speaker to young people.

Joni's approach of "listening" to Scripture is a beautiful example of the idealist's approach to the Crucifixion. It involves listening to the narrative of the Crucifixion at the deepest level of our being, then going a step further and relating the Crucifixion to the situation in which we find ourselves.

Jesus' Approach

One of the ways Jesus used Old Testament events was by bringing them into the present and applying them to a present situation, as Joni did. Take Jesus' temptations in the desert from Luke 4:3–4.

> The Devil said to him, "If you are God's Son, order this stone to turn into bread."
>
> But Jesus answered, "The scripture says, 'Human beings cannot live on bread alone.'"
>
> (see Deuteronomy 8:3)

Jesus responds in the same way to the other temptations (Luke 4:1–13) and other situations. For example, preaching in the synagogue in Nazareth (Luke 4:18), expelling money changers from the Temple (Luke 19:46), and on the cross (Mark 15:34).

Review

By way of a brief review, we see how *Realists*, like Ignatius, tend to function better at the *sense* level. Their approach to the Crucifixion is to make it real by going back in time and reliving it. Hopefully, we will end up saying with the Roman centurion, "This man *was* the Son of God!" Mark 15:39

Intellectuals, like Thomas Aquinas, tend to function at the *mind* or *conscious* level. Their approach is to probe the Crucifixion for its deeper, personal meaning and apply it to their daily lives.

Free spirits, like Francis of Assisi, tend to function better at the *heart* or *subconscious* level. Their approach is to take their lead from the heart and respond to the Crucifixion as the heart dictates.

Idealists, like Augustine, tend to function better at the *soul* or *sanctuary* level in our being. Their approach is to "listen" to God speaking through the Scripture to their situation.

People sometimes ask, "How can I find out my personality type and learn which prayer approach might fit me best?" My answer is that they should try all four approaches in their daily meditation and see which fits best: *Read* the passage and relive the event. *Think*: What thoughts and feelings come to you? *Speak* to Jesus about these thoughts and feelings. *Listen* to what Jesus might say to you in the depths of your heart.

To Ponder and Discuss

1. Which of the four personality types seems to fit me best? Which fits me least? To which prayer phase do I relate best? To which do I relate least? How might I explain this?

2. What is my reaction to the "Principle and Foundation" of *The Spiritual Exercises of St. Ignatius*? If I have problems with one of its five paragraphs, how would I reword it to eliminate the problem?

3. How does the Ignatian prayer approach reflect the Ignatian personality type? How well can I relate to it?

4. How does the legend of Siddhartha's quest for truth reflect the Thomistic personality type and approach to prayer? How do I feel toward the Franciscan prayer approach to the crucifixion of Jesus?

5. How does the monologue of Lt. Kinderman reflect the Franciscan personality type? How does "The Peace Prayer" reflect the personality of Francis?

6. What struck me most about the story of Joni? How does her prayer approach to the Crucifixion reflect the Augustinian temperament and approach to prayer?

Small Group Setting

We Share and Support

Jesus took Peter, John, and James
with him and went up a hill to pray.
Luke 9:28

Grant Teaff was a great football coach at Baylor University. In his book *I Believe*, he recounts an unforgettable event that occurred early in his coaching career at McMurry College in Texas.

One Saturday night, the plane carrying the McMurry College football team had just taken off for its return trip to McMurry. Suddenly, it developed a serious mechanical failure. The plane was thrown into total darkness.

Word was passed that the pilot would attempt a crash landing. It would be especially dangerous because the plane was loaded with fuel. An explosion was likely. One of the players called out, "Coach Teaff, will you lead us in prayer? We're all pretty frightened."

Teaff stood up, rested his hands on the seat in front of him, bowed his head, and prayed fervently. He came right out and asked God to protect the lives of the young men, the coaching staff, and the crew of the plane.

He explained: "Surely, God, you have a plan, a purpose, and a will for our lives. We pray, God, that it not end on this night."

The stewardess then told everyone to prepare for the crash landing. The players bent over, dropped their heads between their legs, and leaned forward in their seats.

A few seconds later, the plane bellied onto the concrete runway. A shower of sparks engulfed it. The right engine exploded into flames. The plane bounced several times, then skidded wildly out of control. Finally, it came to a halt.

The fire chief from the emergency crew that rushed to the scene said he had never seen a plane in such a situation fail to explode. No one was injured.

The next night, Sunday, Teaff and his family were at church. Right in the middle of the services, Teaff got up, left the church, and went to the McMurry field house about a mile away.

He headed directly for the dressing room. This was a room he loved very much. He knelt down in the darkness and began to sob, praying as follows:

God, I know that you have a plan, a purpose, and a will for my life and the lives of these young men. I do not know what it is but I'll . . . try to impress upon the young men I coach this year and forever that there's more to life than just playing football; that you do have a purpose for our lives.

That story illustrates the three settings of prayer: (1) the *personal* setting—alone, as Teaff prayed in the dressing room; (2) the *small-group* setting—in a small group with family or friends, as Teaff prayed with his team on the plane; and (3) the *communal* or *liturgical* setting—with the larger community, as Teaff prayed on Sunday night.

In chapter 1, we explored the *personal* setting, the outer dimension of prayer, and how Jesus prayed in this setting. In chapter 2, we explored the inner dimension of prayer, the three forms it takes, and how Jesus prayed in this setting. In chapter 3, we explored four different personality temperaments and the prayer forms by which they approach God.

In this chapter we will explore the second setting of prayer: the small-group setting with family and friends.

Small-Group Setting

Although the Gospel makes no mention of the family of Jesus praying together, all Jewish families placed a high priority on family prayer. This would be especially true of the Holy Family: Jesus, Mary, and Joseph.

I remember vividly how my own family prayed together when I was a child. There were eight of us. In spite of this rather large number, we set the highest priority on praying together before and after every meal. We also placed a high priority on praying together in the evening, just before the younger children went to bed.

When several of us reached high school age, plays, dances, and games began to cut deeply into our nightly prayer sessions. Eventually, the sessions died out completely.

I'll never forget the summer evening when we revived the practice, even though the entire family was rarely able to gather on any given night.

I remember one night in particular, when my dad happened to be home alone. The rest of the family was at some event. When we returned at a late hour, Dad was still up. When the topic of night prayer surfaced, Dad said, "Go to bed. It's late. At our usual prayer time, I prayed out loud in the name of all of us." That is one of my favorite memories of my father.

Jesus not only prayed together with his family, but also with close friends. Luke recalls one of these times: "Jesus took Peter, John, and James with him and went up a hill to pray." Luke 9:28

Later on, Jesus chose these same three apostles to support him during his prayer in the Garden of Gethsemane, just before his arrest. Matthew 26:37

There are four formats that *interpersonal* or small-group prayer can take.

Guided Prayer

The first format in the interpersonal prayer setting is the one Coach Teaff used with his team just before the crash landing. He led the team, praying out loud while they listened and made his prayer their prayer.

We find Jesus praying in much the same way at the Last Supper, just before his passion. He prayed out loud to his Father, allowing his disciples to make his prayer their own prayer. Jesus prayed:

> Father! . . . I have made you known
> to those you gave me out of the world. . . .
> I gave them the message that you gave me,
> and they received it;
> they know that it is true
> that I came from you,
> and they believe that you sent me. . . .

I will continue to do so, . . .
that the love you have for me
may be in them,
and so that I may also be in them."

John 17:5–8, 26

For want of a better title, we may call this format guided prayer. One person prays out loud; the others simply listen and affirm the prayer in silence.

Silent Prayer

The second format in the interpersonal prayer setting might be called silent prayer. It is when a group gathers and each person prays silently in his or her own way. It is often used in time of tragedy or need. An example is recounted in the book *Years of Upheaval* by former Secretary of State Henry Kissinger.

The incident took place on Wednesday, August 7, 1974. This was the night before President Richard Nixon announced his resignation to the world.

Kissinger was at home having dinner with his wife, Nancy, his children, and columnist Joseph Alsop. At about nine o'clock, the telephone rang. It was President Nixon at the White House; would Kissinger come over immediately?

Kissinger found Nixon slouched in a brown chair. A thin beam of light from a small reading lamp fell on a yellow pad in his lap. The rest of the room was in shadows. The two talked about many things. About midnight, Kissinger got up to leave. Nixon escorted him to the elevator.

Nixon stopped at the door of the Lincoln bedroom and asked him to kneel in silent prayer with him. Kissinger said later that the experience filled him with a "deep sense of awe" and put him at a loss of how to pray. Then, out of nowhere, came this line by the Greek dramatist Aeschylus:

"Pain that cannot forget falls drop by drop upon the heart, and in our despair, against our will, comes wisdom through the awful grace of God."

At a time of personal tragedy, Nixon sought the prayerful support of a close and trusted friend. Jesus prayed in this manner the night before his crucifixion. He

> went with his disciples to a place called Gethsemane, and he said to them, "Sit here while I go over there and pray." He took with him Peter and the two sons of Zebedee. Grief and anguish came over him, and he said to them, "The sorrow in my heart is so great that it almost crushes me. Stay here and keep watch with me."
> Matthew 26:36–38

In time of need, Jesus sought the support of his three closest friends to support him by simply praying in silence.

Dialogue Prayer

The third format of prayer that is used in small groups is a back-and-forth style of prayer. An example of this popular style of prayer is found in the book *Alive* by Piers Paul Read. The situation leading up to the prayer reads like a movie. In fact, it was later made into a movie.

At 3:30 on an October afternoon in 1972, a plane carrying the Uruguayan rugby team from Uruguay to Chile crashed high up in the Andes Mountains. Miraculously, sixteen passengers survived for two months in freezing temperatures without adequate food, shelter, or clothing.

One of the things that contributed greatly to their survival was prayer meetings that they held nightly in the shell of the crashed plane.

Around nine o'clock when the moon dropped below the mountain, they would stop all talking and one of the boys would lead the others in praying the Rosary together. In the Rosary, one person leads and the others respond.

The nightly Rosary sessions became a tremendous source of unity and strength for the boys.

Some who weren't particularly religious began to experience a remarkable presence during these times. An example was a boy named Arturo. He was a rather sullen person. Even his own family found him withdrawn and extremely difficult to communicate with.

One night Arturo surprised everyone by asking to lead the Rosary. As he prayed, he spoke with such deep feeling that the others were struck with a new affection for him.

After the prayer ended, Arturo began to weep softly. "Why are you crying?" someone asked. "Because I feel so close to God," Arturo said.

Eventually, the weather broke and two of the young men managed to descend the mountain. After nine days, they reached help and the remaining fourteen men were rescued.

Shared Prayer

The fourth and final way of praying in a small group is called shared prayer. It is a growing form of prayer among Christians. For many, it has become a life-changing experience. Let's take a detailed look at this prayer format.

Some years back, the *Chicago Tribune* ran a story about businessmen in stressful positions and how they seek the prayerful support of their colleagues.

Headlined "Execs fight stress with prayer," the article described a meeting that was held every Tuesday morning in a seventh-floor private dining room of the New York Stock Exchange.

Slightly before eight o'clock, businessmen started to wander in. They included stockbrokers, investment bankers, floor traders, analysts, and lawyers. Orange juice, sweet rolls, and coffee were served. The atmosphere was warm and friendly.

Promptly at eight o'clock, the men opened their briefcases. Each contained a Bible. A short prayer was then said: "Lord, we ask you to give us the light to see how your word applies to our own hectic business lives."

The prayer was followed by a Bible reading, which was, in turn, followed by a prayerful sharing.

A similar meeting took place on Thursday mornings at One Chase Manhattan Plaza. One businessman said this of these small group meetings: "It's a growing movement. . . . But its growth has purposely been kept quiet." Another executive gave this explanation for the popularity of the meetings:

> Businessmen turn to this because of the desire for fellowship with those who have a common understanding of the pressures of business life. . . . Even one's own family can't appreciate the stresses.

The benefit of the meetings is easy to identify. There are times when we all need the support and sharing of a peer group. Only other businessmen can appreciate the stress that these men are under.

These groups perform yet another function. They support people who are trying to sustain a personal prayer practice.

I became interested in forming such groups when it became clear to me that many people, especially young people, found it hard to persevere in daily prayer. They made heroic efforts, but then tailed off and gave up. The solution? It proved to be a small support group of six to nine people who met on a regular, preferably weekly, basis.

How to Begin

An excellent time to begin a shared prayer group is Lent. Most people are open to doing something special during these six weeks. Another advantage of Lent is that the commitment is for a specified period. This allows members to complete their commitment, discuss the experience, and decide whether they wish to continue beyond Lent. In point of fact, many groups do continue.

Experience has shown that a book of daily meditation exercises is essential for success. It gives the group a track to run on. Ideally the book is based on a passage from the daily Lenten Mass reading and a brief meditation guide for the passage. Members spend ten minutes or so on each of the daily meditations.

Weekly group meetings consist of members sharing with one another *what went on in their minds and their hearts* as they meditated on each daily exercise.

Daily Meditation Exercise

Here is an example of a meditation in the Lenten section of the book *Jesus.*

1. **Reading from the Gospel of the day:** "The Son of man . . . [came] to give his life to redeem many people." Mathew 20:28

2. **Relating reading to daily life:** Little Jason was returning home later and later each afternoon from school. His father lectured him on punctuality, but it made no impact on him. Finally, he told Jason that the next time he was late, he could expect bread and water for supper. Sure enough, the next night Jason was late. When he sat down to supper, he was stunned. On his plate was a single slice of bread. Jason saw that his father meant business. When the punishment had sunk in fully, Jason's father did something Jason never forgot. He gave

Jason his own full plate and took Jason's single slice of bread. That was all Jason's father ate that night.

Years later, Jason said that what his father did at supper that night taught him in the most eloquent way what Jesus did for the human race two thousand years ago.

3. **Applying the bible reading and story to my personal life:** What are some of my thoughts about the story? Can I recall a similar experience from my life?

4. **Concluding thought for the day:** Jesus "endured the suffering that should have been ours, the pain that we should have borne." Isaiah 53:4 (*Jesus: A Contemporary Walk with Jesus,* Mark Link, SJ, page 81.)

Meditation Format

1. *Read* the meditation exercise slowly. When you finish, return to any phrase, sentence, or idea that struck you while reading. (Spend about one minute on this step.)

2. *Think* about the phrase, sentence, or idea that struck you. Might it be addressing something in your life? (Spend about four minutes on this step.)

3. *Speak* to God about your thoughts. Talk to God as you would to a close and trusted friend. (Spend about one minute on this step.)

4. *Listen* to God's response. How might God answer you? Don't force this part of your reflection. Simply rest in God's presence with an open mind and heart. You might wish to begin by saying, "Speak, Lord, your servant is listening." 1 Samuel 3:8 (Spend about four minutes on this step.)

God often speaks to us outside the time of prayer. Listening for God's response begins in prayer and continues subconsciously throughout the day.

Meeting Format

Once the group members have all gathered, the thirty- to forty-minute meeting is called to order. There follows a Call to Prayer. Here's an example that many groups use.

A member lights a candle on the table around which the group is gathered. When the candle is lit, three members read out loud the following:

> **First Reader:** Jesus said, "I am the light of the world, Whoever follows me will have the light of life and never walk in darkness." John 8:12

Second Reader: Lord Jesus, you said that where two or three come together in your name, you are there with them.

The light of this candle symbolizes your presence among us.

Third Reader: And, Lord Jesus, where you are, there, too, are the Father and the Holy Spirit.

And so we begin our meeting in the presence and the name of the Father, the Son, and the Holy Spirit.

Two points about sharing are in order here. First, the group should be patient with the sharing process. It may take a little time to develop, depending on how well the members know, trust, and bond with one another. At first, some may be a bit shy to "share their faith" with others. Be gentle with one another on this point. I personally found that an aid to sharing is to have each member jot down a brief thought that came to them during each daily meditation and simply read it at the meeting. It is a way to start.

Second, the purpose of the meeting is *not* to discuss topics, but to *share* prayer: *what went on in my mind and heart* as I meditated.

Ending the Meeting

The leader ends the meeting promptly at the designated time. (If some members wish to continue to discuss something that came up in the sharing, they should do so after the meeting.)

The meeting concludes with a Call to Mission: a call to witness to Jesus and his teaching. It consists in having three members of the group read the following prayerfully:

First Reader: We conclude our meeting by listening to Jesus say to us what he said to his disciples in his Sermon on the Mount:

Second Reader: "You are like light for the whole world. A city built on a hill cannot be hid. No one lights a lamp and puts it under a bowl; instead it is put on the lampstand, where it gives light for everyone in the house.

In the same way your light must shine before people, so that they will see the good things you do and praise your Father in heaven." Matthew 5:14–16

A member extinguishes the candle that was lit at the beginning of the meeting.

Third Reader: The light of this candle is now extinguished. But the light of Christ in each of us must continue to shine in our lives. Toward this end we pray together the Lord's Prayer: "Our Father . . ."

Points to Ponder and Discuss

1. One of the players called out in the darkness, "Coach Teaff, would you lead us in prayer? We're all pretty frightened." Describe a time when I was in serious danger or some difficult situation.

2. The author says, "I remember vividly how my own family prayed together when I was a child. Do I have any such memories? Describe a prayer experience from my childhood.

3. The author writes, "Dad said, 'Go to bed. It's late. At our usual prayer time, I prayed out loud in the name of all of us.' That is one of my favorite memories of my father." Recall a favorite memory of my father or mother.

4. Kissinger recalled repeating a line that he had memorized in college from the Greek dramatist Aeschylus: "Pain that cannot forget . . ." (page 79) How does it apply to Nixon's situation? Share a line, a poem, or a special prayer that I memorized.

5. If I'm not yet in a prayer group, how interested am I in being in one, or forming one, for six weeks on a trial or experimental basis?

Communal (Liturgical) Setting

CHAPTER 5

We Gather

The believers continued, together
in close fellowship. . . praising God,
and enjoying the good will of all the people.

Acts 2:44–47

Father Walter J. Ciszek spent twenty-three years in Russian prisons and work camps. In his book, *He Leadeth Me*, he writes:

> I have seen . . . prisoners deprive their bodies of needed sleep in order to get up before the rising bell for secret Mass. . . . We would be severely punished if we were discovered saying Mass, and there were always informers. But the Mass to us was always worth the danger and the sacrifice. . . .
>
> We said Mass in drafty storage shacks, or huddled in mud and slush in the corner of a building site foundation. . . . The intensity of

devotion . . . made up for everything; there
were no altars, candles, bells. . . .Yet in these
primitive conditions, the Mass brought you
closer to God than anyone might conceivably
imagine.

In the 1940s and 1950s, Catholics did not eat or
drink after midnight when they were to receive Holy
Communion the following morning. Some prisoners
could not attend these secret Masses, so Father Ciszek
would always consecrate extra hosts and distribute
them when he could. That meant that some prisoners
had to wait until night. Ciszek writes:

Yet these men would actually fast all day long
and do exhausting physical labor without a
bite to eat . . . just to be able to receive the
Holy Eucharist.

This moving story brings us to the third prayer setting, the most important one of all.

Communal Setting: The Mass

The Mass is the center of Catholic life. It expresses,
strengthens, and celebrates our union with Christ and
with one another. It is the focal point of everything we
believe, everything we do, and everything we hope for.

In this liturgical setting, we gather with the larger Christian community just as Jesus used to gather with the larger Jewish community. Let's begin with a bit of background.

In the time of Jesus there were two places where Jews gathered to worship: the synagogue and the temple. The synagogue was mainly a place of prayer and instruction. On the Sabbath, every Jew went to the synagogue to hear God's Word and to pray together as God's people. Luke 4:16-21 The temple, on the other hand, was mainly a place of *sacrifice*. Recall that after the birth of Jesus, Mary and Joseph went to the temple "to offer a sacrifice of a pair of doves." Luke 2:24

This brings us back to the Mass or Lord's Supper. Each Lord's Day, the larger Catholic community gathers around the Lord's table to carry out the command Jesus gave to his disciples at the Last Supper. Luke describes that memorable night:

> Jesus took his place at the table with the apostles. . . . Then he took a piece of bread, gave thanks to God, broke it, and gave it to them, saying, "This is my body, which is given for you. Do this in memory of me." In the same way, he gave them the cup after the supper, saying, "This cup is God's new covenant

sealed with my blood, which is poured out
for you." Luke 22:14, 19–20

The Mass divides into two main parts. The first part
is called the *Liturgy of the Word*—and echoes the
Jewish synagogue service. The second part is called
the *Liturgy of the Eucharist*—and echoes the Jewish
temple service. Acting as a bridge between them are
the Creed (Profession of Faith) and the Prayers of the
Faithful.

Liturgy of the Word

Significantly, both the Liturgy of the Word and the
Liturgy of the Eucharist begin with a procession. The
Liturgy of the Word begins with the carrying of the
book of God's Word to the lectern. The Liturgy of
the Eucharist begins with the carrying of the gifts of
bread and wine to the altar.

The Liturgy of the Word sets the *mood of faith* for
the celebration of the *mystery of faith*—the Liturgy
of the Eucharist. The Liturgy of the Word divides
into two main parts: the gathering rite and the reading rite. This chapter will focus on the first part: the
gathering rite.

Amid music and song, the lector, carrying the
book of God's Word high for all to see, leads the procession of ministers and presider into the assembly.

After greeting the gathering, the presider carries out an important command of Jesus.

We Forgive One Another

Jesus said,

> "If you are about to offer your gift to God at the altar and there you remember that your brother has something against you, leave your gift there in front of the altar, go at once and make peace with your brother, and then come back and offer your gift to God."
>
> Matthew 5:23–24

A sign of authentic Christianity is the readiness of individual Christians to forgive one another. This is not always easy. On our own, we often feel powerless to forgive others as God has forgiven us. An unforgettable episode concerning the command to forgive occurred one day when Peter asked Jesus the question that was on everybody's mind:

> "Lord, if my brother keeps on sinning against me, how many times do I have to forgive him? Seven times?" "No, not seven times," answered Jesus, "but seventy times seven."
>
> Matthew 18:21–22

Peter must have been tempted to say, "You're kidding!" Jesus wasn't kidding. He was simply saying that we must be ready to forgive others in the same unlimited way God is ready to forgive us.

Forgive as God Forgives

The first step in forgiving others as God forgives us is to ask for the *grace* to forgive our enemies. We tend to forget that with each command, God makes available to us the grace to carry it out. Without this grace, we can do nothing. With it "everything is possible for God." Mark 10:27

Our task, then, is to open ourselves to God's grace and cooperate with it. One form of cooperation is to see our enemy in a whole new light: as God sees our enemy. An example will illustrate this point.

In his novel *All Quiet on the Western Front*, Erich Maria Remarque describes a moving scene of forgiveness. It goes something like this. A battle rages between French and German soldiers. A young German soldier lies in a shell hole, taking cover from artillery fire.

Suddenly a French soldier leaps into the same hole, seeking cover also. Before the Frenchman can do anything, the German bayonets him several times. But the French soldier doesn't die immediately. He lingers on.

The young German, still in his teens, studies the eyes of the frightened Frenchman's. He sees his mouth hanging half open, and his lips dry and parched. The sight moves him to pity, and he gives his enemy a drink of water from his own canteen. When the Frenchman finally dies, the young German feels great remorse.

This is the first man he has killed. He wonders what his name is. Seeing a wallet in the dead man's pocket, he removes it reverently. In it are photographs of a woman and a child.

The German soldier is deeply touched. He suddenly realizes that this dying man is not an enemy, but a father and a husband—a human being who loves and is loved just as he himself is.

The German theologian and author Helmut Thielicke was an acquaintance of both President Jimmy Carter and Billy Graham. He wrote a book called *Being a Christian When the Chips Are Down*. In it he analyzes this unforgettable scene.

He asks: "What happened in the shell hole?" Did the German soldier suddenly realize his duty to love his fellow man and to force himself to treat the dying soldier with kindness? Not at all. What happened was this. He suddenly saw the man who was supposed to be his enemy in a whole new light. It was this new vision of him that changed his attitude toward him.

See as Jesus Sees

On the cross, Jesus prayed for his executioners: "Forgive them, Father! They don't know what they are doing." Luke 23:34 Jesus saw his executioners in a much different light than the one in which we see them. Jesus saw beyond the external appearances of his executioners. He saw them as they really were: children of his Father who had lost their way.

If we are to be able to forgive our enemies, we must begin by seeing them in a whole new light. We must try to see them as our heavenly Father sees them. Recall the parable of the prodigal son. Jesus intended the father to mirror his own heavenly Father. Here's how Jesus describes the way the father greets the runaway son:

> [The son] was still a long way from home when his father saw him; his heart was filled with pity, and he ran, threw his arms around his son, and kissed him. Luke 15:20

The father didn't stand at the door and glare at his son as he came down the road. He ran out to him. He did even more—he hugged and kissed him.

Immediately, he ordered the rags on his son's back to be replaced by the "best robe" (festive robe of honor).

The father didn't punish his son. He rejoiced that his son had repented and humbly returned home. The father put "a ring on his finger and shoes on his feet."

The ring probably contained a seal that empowered him to do business in the family's name. The father treats him as if he'd never left home. The shoes were a symbol that he is removed from the status of a slave. He is now a son again. Slaves and family servants went barefoot; sons wore shoes. The Negro spiritual, "Going to Shout All Over God's Heaven" alludes to this symbol:

> I've got shoes, you've got shoes
> All of God's children got shoes
> When I get to Heaven,
> goin' to put on my shoes
> Goin' to walk all over God's Heaven.

Thus the ring and the shoes symbolize the young son's total reunion with the family. The father concludes by instructing the servants to slaughter the fatted calf and prepare a banquet in gratitude for his son's safe return. All is forgiven! It's time to eat, sing, and celebrate.

That brings us to an important second moment in the gathering rite: the singing of the Gloria.

We Begin Our Celebration

The singing of the Gloria. This 1,500-year-old prayer is a song of praise to the Father, Son, and Holy Spirit. It begins with the words the angels sang to the shepherds on the night Jesus was born: "Glory to God in the highest, and peace to his people on earth." Luke 2:14

The Gloria invites us to put ourselves in the presence of God, much as the shepherds left their flocks, hurried through the night, and put themselves in the presence of the infant Son of God. Putting ourselves in the presence of God is the starting point of all prayer and worship.

What do we mean by putting ourselves in God's presence? We consciously reflect on two things: who we are and who God is.

The following example will help to illustrate this point. Admiral Rickover gave President John Kennedy a plaque on which was inscribed "The Breton Fisherman's Prayer: O God, Thy sea is so great and my boat is so small." Kennedy treasured it and kept it on his desk in the Oval Office.

That brief poetic prayer dramatizes the difference between who God is and who I am. It is the difference between an ocean and a drop of water. Without this awareness, worship can be difficult. With it, worship flows naturally and reverently.

We Pray Together

As the last strains of the Gloria fade, the celebrant invites us to join him in praying the opening prayer of Mass. Here is a typical opening prayer:

> Almighty and ever-present Father,
> your watchful care reaches from end to end
> and orders all things in such power
> that even the tensions and tragedies of sin
> cannot frustrate our loving plans.
> Help us to embrace your will,
> give us the strength to follow your call,
> so that your truth may live in our hearts
> and reflect peace to those who believe in your love.
> We ask this in the name of Jesus the Lord.

> Prayer from the Second Sunday of
> Ordinary Time

The congregation responds, "Amen." This word is an ancient Hebrew word that means, "We agree. This is our prayer, too." Our "Amen" in response to the presider's prayer is an affirmation of our solidarity as a community.

With this affirmation, the *gathering rite* concludes. The heart and soul of the Liturgy of theWord—the *reading rite*—follows it. We will discuss the reading rite in the next chapter.

Points to Ponder and Discuss

1. Fr. Ciszek writes "In these primitive conditions the Mass brought us closer to God than anyone can conceivably imagine." Recall a memorable Mass that I experienced.

2. In what two communal settings did Jesus worship? How do the main structures of the Mass echo these two settings? How does the first part of the Mass prepare us for the second part?

3. What insight into forgiving others does the episode in the novel *All Quiet on the Western Front* illustrate? What might keep me from applying this insight to a person who has hurt me badly?

4. What are some parallels between the parable of the prodigal son and the Sacrament of Penance and Reconciliation: examination of conscience, repenting, confessing, amending my life?

5. Explain what the Gloria invites us to do. Why is it so important that I do this? How can the "Breton Fisherman's Prayer" help me to do it?

6. Explain the meaning of *Amen*. What are some reasons why it is so important to pray with a conscious awareness of why I say it?

CHAPTER 6

We Listen

On the Sabbath, Jesus stood and read
from the book of Isaiah. Then he explained
the reading. They all marvelled at his words.
See Luke 4:16–23

Some years ago, the Romanian government freed a number of political and religious prisoners. One was Richard Wurmbrand, a Lutheran pastor. He had spent fourteen years in prison, nearly three of them in solitary confinement. In *In God's Underground*, he describes a scene that took place one day.

A new prisoner named Avram had just arrived. He'd apparently been injured seriously. His upper body was encased in a plaster cast. He sat in silence for a while. Then his hand reached beneath the plaster cast and drew out a book. Avram began to read it. Wurmbrand writes:

> None of us had seen a book of any kind for years. Avram lay there quietly turning the

pages, until he became conscious of the eager
eyes fixed on him. . . . "It's the Gospel according to John," he said.

Avram had managed to conceal the Gospel under his
cast at the time of his arrest. He held out the book.
Wurmbrand says:

> I took the little book in my hands as if it were
> a live bird. No life-saving drug could have
> been more precious to me.

From that day on, the tattered little book went from
hand to hand among the prisoners. Many learned it
by heart and each day they would discuss it among
themselves.

It takes a story like that to rekindle our apprecia-
tion of what a great gift the Bible is.

God's Word

Ancient Jewish kings used to keep the sacred scroll of
God's word near the throne. Jewish generals used to
carry it into battle. Today, Jewish congregations carry
the scroll in procession around the synagogue before
reading from it.

In his book *The Jewish Jesus*, Robert Aron describes the procession, saying that everyone crowds in upon the scroll. All try to touch it with the end of their *tallith* or prayer shawl. Then they kiss the part of the shawl that touched the scroll.

All of this shows the profound reverence Jews have for God's Word. Reading it is the most solemn moment of the synagogue service.

St. Luke describes that moment when the synagogue leaders invited Jesus to read. He unrolled the scroll of Isaiah to the place where it is written:

> "The spirit of the Lord is upon me, because he has chosen me to . . . announce that that the time has come when the Lord will save his people."
>
> Jesus rolled up the scroll, gave it back to the attendant, and sat down. All the people in the synagogue had their eyes fixed on him, as he said to them, "This passage of scripture has come true today, as you heard it being read."
>
> They were all well impressed with him and . . . the eloquent words that he spoke.
>
> Luke 4:18–22

We Read God's Word

The reading of God's Word is the heart and soul of the Liturgy of the Word. Its format is similar to the one described by St. Luke. The first reading on Sundays is normally from the Old Testament.

Bishop Fulton Sheen used to compare the Old Testament to a radio. Listening to it, we hear the Word of God. The New Testament, on the other hand, is like television. Listening to it, we not only hear the Word of God, but we see it come alive and walk around in the person of Jesus.

The Old Testament is the foundation upon which the New Testament rests. It prepared the way for our understanding of everything Jesus said and did.

If we had only the New Testament, it would be like tuning into a TV mystery story in the middle of it. If we had only the Old Testament, it would be like watching the first half of a mystery story, but not watching the last half.

St. Augustine made this comparison between the two Testaments. "In the Old Testament, the New Testament lies concealed. In the New Testament, the Old Testament is revealed."

In other words, the Old Testament is like a tulip bulb. Concealed within it is a beautiful flower. The New Testament is like the flower that emerges from the bulb.

First Reading

At Sunday Mass, the first reading is usually from the Old Testament. It is followed by an appropriate psalm, called a *responsorial psalm*.

Someone once said that if the entire Old Testament got lost except for the book of Psalms, we could recover much of its spirit and content from the book of Psalms alone. This is because the book of Psalms is a combination songbook and prayer book. It puts into song and prayer form the important events and fundamental beliefs and practices of God's chosen people. Thus the *responsorial psalm* acts as a kind of meditation on the first reading.

Second Reading

On Sunday, the second reading is normally from one of the letters of Paul or another apostle. These letters deal with practical, everyday problems. They apply the teachings of Jesus to daily life.

Gospel Reading

The final reading is from one of the Gospels. It is the most important reading. That's why we stand and introduce it with a *Gospel Acclamation*. It is a kind of *preview* of the reading. For example the acclamation for the gospel reading for Midnight Mass on Christmas reads:

> Good News and great joy to all the world;
> today is born our Savior, Christ the Lord.

Many people trace the Sign of the Cross on their forehead, lips, and heart as the Gospel reading is announced by the lector. They accompany the tracing with these words, "May the Word of God always be in my mind, on my lips, and in my heart."

We Listen to God's Word

Years ago there was a Broadway play called *The Royal Hunt of the Sun.* It concerned Spain's conquest of the Indians in Peru in the sixteenth century. One scene was especially moving. An Indian chief was handed a Bible and told that it was God's Word. The chief put it to his ear. When he heard nothing, he felt duped and slammed the Bible down in anger. The scene makes us ask: "How ought we to listen to God's Word at Mass?"

Both St. Augustine and the Second Vatican Council said: "When the sacred Scriptures are read and explained, it is Christ who speaks to us." Both of them are merely echoing the words of Jesus himself, who promised his apostles: "Whoever listens to you listens to me." Luke 10:16

With this in mind, we must first listen to the reading with faith. Jesus himself assures us that in some mysterious way he is speaking directly to us. Thus, a third-century Christian homilist, Origen, used to tell his congregations:

> You receive the body of the Lord with special care and reverence, lest the smallest crumb of the consecrated gift fall to the floor. You should receive the Word of the Lord with equal care and reverence, lest the smallest word of it fall to the floor and be lost.

Second, we must take to heart what Jesus might be saying to us personally. We ask ourselves, for example, "What might Jesus be saying to me about my life through this particular parable or passage?"

Third, we ask ourselves, "How might I put the passage into practice right now in my life?"

Some years ago, Father George Anderson formed a prayer group with some inmates at the maximum security prison at Rikers Island, New York.

One night they were reading and reflecting on the parable of the Good Samaritan. It was a cold night in March and there was little heat in the room.

One inmate had on only a T-shirt and a pair of pants. He was shivering visibly. Another inmate named Richard was wrapped in two blankets.

Suddenly, Richard got up, walked over to the shivering inmate, and put one of the blankets around him. Richard had heard God's word not only with his ears but also with his heart. He applied it lovingly to life.

The Homily

Peter, Paul, and Mary was the name of a popular singing group some years ago. One member of the group, Noel "Paul" Stookey, felt a void in his life in spite of their success. One night he talked to composer and singer Bob Dylan about it.

Dylan recommended that he go back to his school to reconnect with his *human* roots and begin to read the New Testament to reconnect with his *spiritual* roots. Stookey wrote later:

> I started reading the New Testament. Dylan was right because I began discovering that all the truths I sought were contained in the life of this man. . . . It was fantastic. He set a good example, but it never occurred to me that he could really be the Son of God. . . . I started carrying the Scriptures around with me. . . . It was almost like having a brother with you.

Then one night backstage during a concert in Austin, Texas, Paul happened to be talking to a young man about the Scriptures. Paul says:

"Somehow this guy made all the reading in Scriptures make sense." Then right there in the midst of all the concert activity, the two young men began to pray together over the Scriptures. That night changed Paul's life forever.

Paul's experience illustrates an important point. It helps to have some explanation and motivation when it comes to understanding and putting into practice the Word of God we have heard read. This is the role of the homilist.

The homilist has studied the Scriptures carefully and prayed over how they apply to everyday life. He also has been given a special grace by virtue of his ordination as a priest or a deacon that enables him to speak in the name of Jesus.

The homily may not always be what it should be. Not all homilists are born to be dynamic speakers. And sometimes preparation suffers. But if we listen with faith, an open heart, and an open mind, God will speak to us in his own way.

The Creed

The Creed is the bridge between the Liturgy of the Word and the Liturgy of the Eucharist. Let's introduce it with a question. If someone offered you a million dollars if you could tell him in a complete and correct way—while standing on one foot—what the Catholic faith was all about, could you do it?

As they say, "It would be a piece of cake." All you would have to do is to recite the Creed, as we do every Sunday. The Creed is a concise statement of what Christians believe. That's why we stand when he recite it, for if we don't stand for something, we fall for everything.

Prayers of the Faithful

The Creed is followed by the Prayers of the Faithful. Jesus said, "For those who ask will receive, and those who seek will find, and the door will be opened to anyone who knocks." Luke 11:10

In the spirit of these words of Jesus, we place before our heavenly Father our needs and the needs of our world. When you think about it, it is fitting that the Liturgy of the Word should end with prayers not only for ourselves but for the whole world. Why? In his unforgettable Sermon on the Mount, Jesus said to his followers: "You are like light for the whole world." Matthew 5: 14 That means that we have a tremendous responsibility toward the world. Jesus commissioned us to be its light.

The Prayers of the Faithful are one of the ways by which we can respond to this awesome responsibility. We might approach the Prayers of the Faithful by asking ourselves this question: "What bad news in our nation or the world needs to be turned into good news, and for what good news do we need to give thanks to God?"

And so the Liturgy of the Word ends by reminding us of our great responsibility and giving us an opportunity to do something about it.

Points to Ponder and Discuss

1. What is one of my favorite Gospel stories? Parables? Passages?

2. Augustine said: "In the Old Testament, the New Testament lies concealed. In the New Testament, the Old Testament is revealed." How might I explain the meaning of this statement to someone unfamiliar with the Old and the New Testament?

3. Why is a psalm an appropriate response to the Old Testament reading?

4. What is the meaning of the tracing of the Sign of the Cross on my forehead, lips, and heart?

5. The author says, "Richard had heard God's word not only with his ears but also with his heart." How do I listen with my heart?

6. What was one of the best homilies I have ever heard? If I were asked to give a homily, what topic would I choose? Why this one?

7. If my son, daughter, or friend complained about a homily they heard, what advice would I give him or her? To what extent do I agree with the author's advice on this point?

CHAPTER 7

We Break Bread
and Go Forth

Because there is one loaf of bread,
all of us, though many, are one body,
for we all share in the same loaf.

1 Corinthians 10:17

Two novels by Elie Wiesel, *The Town Beyond the Wall* and *A Beggar in Jerusalem*, illustrate the power of friendship. In both cases, the power flows not from the physical presence of the friend but from the *memory* of an *absent* friend.

In the first novel, Michael survives torture because his friend Pedro lives in his memory. In the second novel, David survives difficult trials for the same reason: a close friend lives in his memory.

In *The Living Reminder*, Henri J. M. Nouwen points out that memory not only connects us with our past but is also a source of strength and life in the present.

According to Nouwen, Wiesel's novels touch not only on a profound truth, but also on a

> mystery deeply anchored in the biblical tradition. . . . To remember is not simply to look back at past events; more importantly, it is to bring these events into the present and celebrate them here and now. For Israel, remembrance means participation.

It was this special "remembering" that Jesus had in mind when he told his apostles, "Do this in memory of me." Luke 22:19 He gave future generations a way to participate in the mystery of the Last Supper just as truly as the apostles did on that historical night in Jerusalem.

The Liturgy of the Eucharist

In the previous chapter, we saw how the Liturgy of the Word set the "mood of faith" for celebrating the "mystery of faith": the Liturgy of the Eucharist.

The Liturgy of the Word begins with the presider and other ministers processing up to the sanctuary. The lector elevates the book of God's Word for all to see. The Liturgy of the Eucharist begins in a similar way. Representatives of the community process up to the sanctuary, carrying the gifts of bread and wine to the presider at the table of the Lord.

The presider receives the gifts and prepares them for the mystery at hand. He invites everyone to pray "that our sacrifice may be acceptable to God, the almighty Father." He concludes the preparation rite praying:

> Lord, accept the gifts of your Church.
> May this eucharist
> help us grow in holiness and faith.
> We ask this in the name of Jesus the Lord.
>> Prayer from the Fifteenth Sunday of
>> Ordinary Time

The Eucharistic Prayer

Now all is ready for our remembrance of the Last Supper. The Eucharistic Prayer is opened with a *Preface*.

After extending his hands, the presider exhorts everyone to "Lift up your hearts" and "Let us give thanks to the Lord, our God." A brief prayer follows, after which everyone joins the presider and the choir singing joyously:

> Holy, holy, holy Lord,
> God of power and might,
> Heaven and earth are full of your glory.

Hosanna in the highest.
Blessed is he who comes in the name of the Lord.
Hosanna in the highest.

The words "Holy, holy, holy" recall Isaiah's vision of heaven. The Lord is seated on a throne and flaming creatures cry: "Holy, holy, holy!" Isaiah 6:3 The words "Hosanna in the highest . . . Blessed is he who comes in the name of the Lord" recall the first Palm Sunday. As Jesus entered Jerusalem, an enthusiastic crowd "spread their cloaks on the road, while others cut branches from the trees and strewed them on the road" as they cried out:

> "Hosanna to the Son of David; blessed is he who comes in the name of the Lord; hosanna in the highest." Matthew 21:9 NAB

The Supper Narrative

The presider extends his hands and prays: "Lord, you are holy indeed, the fountain of all holiness."

Then placing both hands over the bread and wine, he prays solemnly and reverently:

> Let your Spirit come upon these gifts to make them holy, so that they may become

for us the body and blood of our Lord, Jesus Christ.

While saying "the body and blood," he makes the Sign of the Cross over the bread and wine. Then he continues, saying:

> Before he was given up to death, a death he freely accepted he took bread and gave you thanks. He broke the bread, gave it to his disciples, and said: "Take this all of you and eat it: this is my body which will be given up for you."

Then, he elevates the sacramental body of Christ for all to see and reverence. He returns it to the paten, takes the chalice, and says:

> When supper was ended, he took the cup. Again he gave you thanks and praise, gave the cup to his disciples, and said: "Take this all of you, and drink from it: this is the cup of my blood, the blood of the new and everlasting covenant. It will be shed for you and for all so that sins may be forgiven. Do this in memory of me."

After elevating the chalice for all to see, he returns it to the altar.

Reflection on the Gospel Narrative

The *prayer over the bread* recalls the day that Jesus made this awesome promise to his followers:

> "I am the living bread that came down from heaven. If anyone eats this bread, he will live forever. The bread that I will give you is my flesh which I give so that the world may live."
> John 6:51

The *prayer over the cup* recalls the "new covenant" that the Lord promised through Jeremiah. It is now being inaugurated by Jesus. Jeremiah 31:31 In a similar way, the words "sealed with my blood" recall God's covenant with Israel at Mount Sinai.

On that occasion Moses splashed blood on the people and said, "This is the blood that seals the covenant which the LORD made with you." Exodus 24:8

Finally, the words "my body given for you" and "my blood shed for you" speak of sacrifice. The word *sacrifice* is not well understood today. To get a glimpse of its meaning, consider a story that Blessed Mother Teresa of Calcutta told when she received the Nobel Peace Prize in Oslo, Norway. She said:

> The other day I received $15 from a man who has been on his back for twenty years.

The only part of his body that he can move is his right hand. The only companion he enjoys is smoking. And he said to me: "I do not smoke for one week and I send you the money."

It must have been a terrible *sacrifice* for him. And with that money I bought bread and gave it to those who are hungry. He was giving, and the poor were receiving.

And so the Last Supper is closely linked with Jesus' sacrifice on the cross. Thus St. Paul writes:

> The cup we use in the Lord's Supper and for which we give thanks to God: when we drink from it, we are sharing in the blood of Christ. And the bread we break: when we eat it, we are sharing in the body of Christ.
>
> 1 Corinthians 10:16

The supper narrative is followed by everyone joining with the choir in song to proclaim the great *mystery of our faith*:

> Christ has died,
> Christ is risen,
> Christ will come again.

Memorial Prayer

Next, the presider extends his hands and addresses the Father. He begins praying reverently: "In memory of his death and resurrection, we offer you, Father, this life-giving bread, this saving cup."

The prayer affirms that every sacrifice of the Mass makes "sacramentally present under the species of bread and wine Christ's body and blood, his sacrifice offered on the cross once and for all." In other words, "The sacrifice of Christ and the sacrifice of the Eucharist are *one single sacrifice.*" *Catechism of the Catholic Church*, paragraphs 1353 and 1367

A series of petitions to the Father follow. Among them we ask our Father's blessing on all our brothers and sisters, both living and dead.

The *memorial prayer* concludes with the presider elevating the chalice and host and singing:

> Through him, with him, and in him, in the unity of the Holy Spirit, all glory and honor is yours almighty Father, for ever and ever.

The congregation responds with a resounding "Amen." From earliest times, Christians have called this amen the Great Amen. In some churches, it literally explodes. Trumpets, trombones, and the voices of the people make it an unforgettable moment in the celebration of the Lord's Supper.

It is a moment of joy. It is a moment of celebration as the voices of Christians down through the ages join in one voice to praise the Father for his incredible blessings given us through, with, and in Christ.

Communion Service

The communion service begins with everyone standing and praying the Lord's Prayer. Let me digress for a minute to say something about this remarkable prayer, which Jesus taught us.

It was a hot Sabbath afternoon and Dorothy Dawes was standing on a beach on the Sea of Galilee. Swarms of little children were all about. One friendly child came up to Dorothy and identified himself as Eliezer. Then off he ran. "Moments later, he had made his way up to a makeshift high dive. There he was calling at the top of his voice to his father to watch: '*Ab-ba! Ab-ba!*'"

Abba is the same word that Jesus used to address his heavenly Father. It is a word of warmth, trust, and affection, akin to our word *daddy*. It is this word that Jesus taught us to use in addressing "Our Father" in the Lord's Prayer.

The Lord's Prayer, with its petition "give us our daily bread" makes a perfect prayer for preparing for communion.

After the Lord's Prayer comes the sign of peace. From the earliest times, Christians have always greeted one another affectionately. St. Paul writes to the Corinthians, "Greet one another with the kiss of peace." 1 Corinthians 16:20

The sign of peace, is accompanied by the words, "May the peace of Christ be with you." The Hebrew word *shalom*, translated into English as "peace," means much more than just the absence of war, strife, or conflict. Actually, it has no English word that is its equivalent.

Maybe the closest we can come to it is to call it the fullness of every good thing: forgiveness, love, joy, happiness. It is wishing one another every blessing we can wish for but only God can give.

Breaking of Bread

The sign of peace is followed by the breaking of the bread. From early times breaking bread together was a sign of unity. This is especially the case when it comes to the Lord's Supper. St. Paul explains the unity connection this way: "Because there is one loaf of bread, all of us, though many, are one body, for we all share in the same loaf." 1 Corinthians 10:17

That brings us back to the big difference between the Last Supper and ordinary suppers. At ordinary suppers, what we eat becomes part of us. At the Lord's Supper, we become part of what we eat: the mystical body of the risen Christ.

By offering himself to us in the form of food, Jesus shows his desire to be one with us. By accepting Jesus' offering of himself in the form of food, we show our desire to be one with him. By sharing the Eucharist with others, we show our desire to become one with them.

Thus Jesus prayed at the Last Supper: "I pray that they may all be one. Father! May they be in us, just as you are in me and I am in you. May they be one, so that the world will believe that you sent me."
John 17:21

The breaking of bread at the Lord's Supper once took a long time. People filled the time with song. This explains the singing of the "Lamb of God."

Today we still sing it, even though we use small hosts instead of breaking bread into smaller pieces for the whole congregation.

Communion

The eucharistic meal at Mass has always been a special moment for the Christian community. It is also a special moment for presiders and for Extraordinary Ministers of Holy Communion. A priest describes why:

> People come up, hundreds of them: grand-
> mas and grandpas with canes, . . . mothers
> and fathers holding their children, careworn
> faces, and happy faces—Suddenly in the
> midst of it all, a wave of gladness comes over
> me. I'm so very glad to be here today. . . . For
> a few moments I choke up and can't say the
> simplest words: "The Body of Christ."
>
> John Eagan, SJ, *A Traveler Toward the Dawn*

That brings us to our own reception of communion.
The minister holds up the body of Christ, saying,
"The Body of Christ." We respond, "Amen." We do
the same in receiving the chalice containing the Blood
of Christ. We then return to our seat to commune
with Jesus in whatever the Holy Spirit leads us.

Reflection after Receiving Communion

Not long ago a woman was asked, "What do you do
after receiving communion?" She explained that she
used to close her eyes and say a prayer of thanks-
giving. Then one Sunday something happened to
change all that. She explains it this way:

> I, unintentionally, raised my head, opened
> my eyes, and realized for the first time that all

these people were becoming one—united in Christ through their reception of his Body.

She, then added,

> For me Mass had always been a very private time. But since that Sunday, the feeling of family has greatly enhanced my worship at Mass. I view what happened to me that Sunday as a gift of God.
>
> Name withheld, *Catholic Digest*

The woman's response is in perfect accord with what Jesus prayed for at the Last Supper:

> "I pray . . . for those who believe in me. . . . I pray that they may all be one. Father! May they be in us, just as you are in me and I am in you. May they be one, . . . just as you and I are one." John 17:20–22

Concluding Rite

After all have received communion, the singing subsides, and silence reigns for a few minutes. It is a special moment. Then the presider prays:

Lord,
you have nourished us with bread from heaven.
Fill us with your Spirit,
and make us one in peace and love.
We ask this through Christ our Lord.

Prayer from the Second Sunday in Ordinary Time

The presider blesses us and charges us to "Go in peace to love and serve the Lord." Commenting on the concluding rite, someone said:

The holiest moment in the church service is the moment when God's people—strengthened by preaching and the sacrament—go out the church door into the world to be Church. Ernest Southcourt

Important Reminder

After instituting the Mass at the Last Supper, Jesus said to his apostles, "Do this is in memory of me."

Referring to these words of Jesus, St. Paul said, "This means that every time you eat this bread and drink from this cup you proclaim the Lord's death until he comes." 1 Corinthians 11:26

Henri Nouwen spells out the point of St. Paul's words in *The Living Reminder*, saying:

> We eat bread, but not enough to take our hunger away; we drink wine, but not enough to take our thirst away; we read from a book, but not enough to take our ignorance away.

Nouwen goes on to say that the inability of these three actions to take away or satisfy our desires speaks of God's absence. Jesus has not yet returned in glory. Thus, paradoxically, at Mass we celebrate both a presence and an absence.

> The great temptation of ministry is to celebrate only the presence of the Lord while forgetting his absence. Often the minister is most concerned to make the people glad. . . . But in this way everything gets filled up and there is no empty space left for the affirmation of our basic lack of fulfillment. . . .
>
> Therefore every time ministers call their people around the table, . . . they call them to experience not only the Lord's presence but his absence as well; they call them to mourning

as well as to feasting, to sadness as well as to
joy, to longing as well as satisfaction.

The kingdom of God is only in process; it is not yet
complete. The vine is growing; but is has not yet
borne its fruit.

Points to Ponder and Discuss

1. Recall a memorable event in my life. How does this memory differ from the biblical understanding of liturgical remembering, e.g. Jesus' words, "Do this in memory of me"?

2. Recall a major sacrifice I was asked to make. What helped or motivated me to make it?

3. How does Jesus' "giving of himself under the form of food" make the reception of Communion an intimate expression of what Christianity with Jesus and with one another should be?

4. What makes the concluding rite of Mass a holy moment? In what sense is the celebration of Mass, paradoxically, a time of joy and a time of longing?

5. If a son, daughter, or friend told me that he or she got little out of the Mass, what might I say to him or her? What do I get out of Mass?

CHAPTER 8

We Break through the Barriers

Jesus said to Peter, . . . "Are you asleep? . . .
Pray that you will not fall into temptation.
The spirit is willing, but the flesh is weak."

Mark 14:37–38

There comes a time in our spiritual journey to God when our fervor and enthusiasm seem to dim and grow cold. It happens to almost everyone who takes the spiritual life seriously. John of the Cross called this period the "moment of flatness."

Commenting on it, Fr. John Canary says, "This experience is not to be confused with depression or burnout. In burnout or depression, we not only lose enthusiasm but energy as well. We shut down."

This is not the case with the moment of flatness. During it, we keep functioning, but with little or no satisfaction. Our spiritual life, especially our prayer, becomes a chore or leaves us cold.

This experience occurs in other areas of life as well. What is at stake here is not a matter of recovering our old zip. Rather, it's a matter of maturity, a matter of purifying our love and our motives.

Take Marriage

There comes a time in every marriage when a couple must make the transition from romantic love to committed love. When it comes to romantic love, the rewards are built-in; we enjoy giving ourselves to our spouse.

But the day comes when the built-in rewards of romantic or young love no longer function as they once did. When this happens, it is a sign that love is calling us to a deeper level of maturity and motivation. It is an essential phase of growth and health wherever commitment and dedication are involved, be it marriage, prayer, or friendship.

Memorable Insight

I'll never forget an episode that took place in a faith-sharing group one morning in Chicago. Nine businessmen and I had been meditating daily and meeting weekly for over three years.

On this particular morning, one of the men explained to the others that he was experiencing a dry period in his prayer. Two others followed suit. At this point, one of the members made an invaluable contribution. In the process of sharing it with you, I'll expand on some of his remarks. He said:

> I grew up on a farm in Wisconsin. Let me tell you about the corn-planting season. The first thing we did after planting corn was to pray for rain—lots of rain. The rain came down; and the corn came up. It was a beautiful sight. You felt like singing and dancing, the way Gene Kelly did in the movie *Singin' in the Rain*.
>
> Then we did something weird—I mean weird, weird. We prayed for a period of "stress and dryness." (Those were his exact words.) The reason we did this is that if the corn got too much rain, its roots would spread out horizontally and would not be forced to go down vertically in their search for water.
>
> If this happened, the corn was in trouble when the dry summer season arrived. The roots wouldn't know where to find water. As a result you ended up with an inferior crop.

Then he made his point, saying:

> God does something like this to us. Up until
> now God has made our prayer an exciting
> experience. It's now time to drive our spiri-
> tual roots down through the "feeling" level
> to the "faith" level. Unless this happens, we
> end up not bearing much fruit.
>
> If we pray simply because it gives us a warm
> glow, then our prayer is in danger of becom-
> ing just another form of self-indulgence. In
> other words, when the built-in rewards of
> daily prayer are no longer there, as they once
> were, we must find motives greater than our
> own satisfaction or inner excitement to con-
> tinue praying.

Blessing from God

Not one man in that faith group that morning ever
forgot that simple explanation. They all knew that
the dryness and darkness they were experiencing was
actually a blessing from God, helping them to mature
spiritually.

What should be our spiritual strategy when this
experience of flatness invades our prayer life? John of

the Cross tells us to stay with our spiritual routines. Above all, we should not stop praying. To do so would be to frustrate the process of driving our spiritual tap roots down through the feeling level to the faith level.

Important Clarification

Our spiritual life and our faith are like the sun. Sometimes it shines brightly. At other times, it seems to go behind a cloud and leaves us in varying levels of darkness. There are three reasons for this darkness or flatness: human nature, ourselves, and God.

First, the darkness or flatness may stem from the mood swings of our human nature. On some days, life is a dream; on other days, it is a drag. We may experience something similar with our faith. Mood swings can vary in intensity from person to person, but they simply go with the territory of being human. Welcome to the human race!

Second, darkness and flatness may be of our own making. We may neglect our faith and spiritual life and let them grow weak from sin or lack of spiritual nourishment. Just as our body grows weak from abuse or lack of proper nourishment, so do our faith and our spiritual life.

Third, our periods of faith darkness may be trace-able to God, in this sense: Experience shows that

God offers us the opportunity to use the ailments, trials, and tragedies of our daily life to grow better rather than to grow bitter. So, too, experience shows that God can use the ailments, trials, and tragedies of our spiritual life to deepen and mature our faith and spiritual life. God's grace is always at our disposal. We need only open our hearts to it.

Dark Night

This brings us back to the period of flatness—and to a phenomenon that happens to some people during it. The period of flatness can intensify into what John of the Cross calls the "dark night of the Spirit." In other words, the darkness can become so intense that we reach the point where we feel totally abandoned by God.

A good example of this is Mother Teresa during the latter half of her life. She felt abandoned by Jesus. The postulator for her beatification said, "Darkness was her traveling companion."

The abandonment she—and others—have felt is akin to the same feeling of abandonment that Jesus felt on the cross. Saint Mark writes: "At three o'clock, Jesus cried out with a loud shout, *"Eloi, Eloi, lema sabachthani?"* which means, "My God, my God, why did you abandon me?" Mark 15:34

Some people ask, "Where is God during this experience of total abandonment?" Perhaps the best way to answer that question is with a true story.

Author Marion Bond West lost her father when she was four. This necessitated that her mother get a job to generate income. Each morning, Marion's mother would leave her with their neighbor and go to work. Each noon, her mother would hurry back to eat lunch with Marion. When her mother prepared to leave after lunch, however, Marion would grow hysterical. She didn't want her mother to leave.

One day Marion's mother stopped coming back to have lunch with her. Marion wondered why. Did her mother still love her? Years later, Marion learned the truth: Her mother had gone home each noon. She had sat at the kitchen window eating lunch, watching Marion play next door. All the while, she longed to hold Marion in her arms.

Marion's mother wasn't absent at all. She was there all the while, close enough to touch Marion. But for Marion's own good and growth, she withheld her presence.

Similarly, God withholds his presence from us because he knows it is time for our spiritual growth to develop and mature. God is intimately present, but withholds his presence from us. God knows it's time for our spiritual growth to reach a new level of maturity.

Jesus Is Our Model

So how should we respond at this time? During his agony in the garden, Jesus turned his will over to his Father, praying: "Father, if you will, take this cup of suffering away from me. Not my will, however, but your will be done." Luke 22:42

During his agony on the cross, Jesus felt totally abandoned by his Father. So what did he do? He trusted his Father totally, saying, "In your hands I place my Spirit!" Luke 23:46

In the movie, *A Patch of Blue*, a blind girl asks her old, irritable grandfather, "What is green like?" He snaps, "Green is green, stupid. Now stop asking questions." This exchange is followed by a touching scene in which the blind girl presses a leaf against her cheek, hoping to "feel" the color green.

When it comes to God, many of us are like the blind girl. We want to "feel" God's presence when we pray, and we become depressed if we don't. Take Keith Miller. In his book *The Taste of New Wine*, he writes:

> So much of my life I had been a spiritual sensualist, always wanting to feel God's presence

in my prayers and being depressed when I didn't.

Then it dawned on Miller one day that feeling is not the point of prayer. If we pray to feel a "high," we risk turning prayer into an act of indulging ourselves rather than an act of loving God.

Awareness of God's presence in prayer is a gift from God. If God gives it to us—as he does from time to time—then we need do no more than remain in the spiritual glow of God's presence. Any effort on our part to make ourselves feel God's presence is nearly always wrong.

One Final Point

Experience shows that we receive the "grace" or "fruit" of prayer after a period of prayer more often than during it. This underscores an important point: In many ways our time of prayer is a seed-planting time. As we all know, it takes time for seeds to germinate, grow, and bear fruit. The point? Though we "feel" nothing during the time of prayer, the truth is that much is happening.

Let us conclude by joining the psalmist in praising and giving thanks to God for God's many gifts to us. One of the greatest gifts is prayer, which allows us to call upon God to help us change ourselves and our world.

> I praise you Lord, because you have saved me. . . .
> I cried to you for help, O Lord my God,
> and you healed me. . . .
> I was on my way to the depths below,
> but you restored my life.

> Sing praise to the Lord,
> all his faithful people!
> Remember what the Holy One has done,
> and give him thanks! . . .
> Tears may flow in the night,
> but joy comes in the morning.

> You have changed my sadness
> into a joyful dance;
> you have taken away my sorrow
> and surrounded me with joy.
> So I will not be silent;
> I will sing praise to you.
> Lord, you are my God;
> I will give you thanks forever.

Psalm 30:1, 2–4, 5, 11–12

Points to Ponder and Discuss

1. To what extent do I think young couples about to marry are aware of the eventual "moment of flatness" that invades almost every marriage and what its purpose is?

2. To what extent have I experienced what the businessmen experienced in their prayer life? What was its purpose?

3. What advice or strategy does John of the Cross recommend to those who begin to experience the "moment of flatness"?

4. Of the three possible reasons for the entry of flatness or darkness into our prayer life, which do I think is the most prevalent?

5. How does the "dark night of the spirit" differ from the "moment of flatness"? When did Jesus experience a feeling of abandonment by the Father and how did he respond to it?

6. What is the point of the Marion Bond West story?

7. What point does Keith Miller make when it comes to "feeling" God's presence?

8. Explain the point the author is making when he writes, "In many ways our time of prayer is a seed-planting time?"

Bibliography

Aron, Robert. *The Jewish Jesus.* Translated by Agnes H. Forsyth and Anne-Marie de Commaille and in collaboration with Horace T. Allen, Jr. Maryknoll, NY: Orbis Books, 1971

Barclay, William. *The Gospel of Luke.* Louisville, KY: Westminister John Knox Press, 2001.

Basset, Fr. Bernard, SJ. *How to Pray.* Waldwick, NJ: Arena Letters, 1975.

Blatty, William Peter. *Legion: A Novel.* New York: Simon and Schuster, 1983.

Buckingham, Jamie. *Power for Living.* West Palm Beach, FL: Arthur S. DeMoss Foundation, 1983.

Catechism of the Catholic Church: revised in accordance with the official Latin text promulgated by Pope John Paul II. 2nd ed. Vatican City: Libreria Editrice Vaticana, 1997.

Ciszek, Walter J. *He Leadeth Me.* With Daniel L. Flaherty. San Francisco: Ignatius Press, 1995.

Donnelly, Doris. *Putting Forgiveness into Practice.* Allen, TX: Tabor Publishing, 1982.

Doré, Derrell John. "Trapped at the Bottom of the Sea." In *The Guideposts Treasury of Love.* Garden Cityl, NY: Doubleday, 1981.

Eagan, John, SJ. *A Traveler toward the Dawn.* Chicago: Loyola University Press, 1990.

Evely, Louis. *Our Prayer.* Translated by Paul Burns. New York: Herder and Herder, 1970.

Gallwey, W. Timothy. *The Inner Game of Tennis.* New York: Random House, 1974.

Griffin, Emilie. *Turning: Reflections on the Experience of Conversion.* Garden City, NY: Doubleday, 1980.

Hertz, Emmanuel. *Lincoln Talks: A Biography in Anecdote*, 559. Collected, collated, and edited by Emanuel Hertz. New York: The Viking Press, 1939.

Keirsey, David, and Marilyn Bates. *Please Understand Me: Character & Temperament Types.* Del Mar, CA: Prometheus Nemesis, 1978.

Kissinger, Henry. *Years of Upheaval.* Boston: Little, Brown, 1982.

Link, Mark, SJ. *Jesus 2000: A Contemporary Walk with Jesus*, 81. Allen, TX: Thomas More, 1997.

Matheson, Richard. "The Traveller." *Third from the Sun*. New York: Bantam 1294, 1955.

Merton, Thomas. *The Seven Storey Mountain*. New York: Harcourt, Brace, 1948.

Michael, Chester P., and Marie C. Norrisey. *Prayer and Temperament: Different Prayer Forms for Different Personality Types*. Charlottesville, VA: Open Door, 1984.

Miller, Keith. *The Taste of New Wine*. Waco, TX: Word Books, 1965.

Nigro, Armand, SJ. "Prayer: A Personal Response to God's Presence."

Read, Piers Paul. *Alive: The Store of the Andes Survivors*. Philadelphia: Lippincott, 1974.

Remarque, Erich Maria. *All Quiet on the Western Front*. Boston: Little, Brown, 1975.

Tada, Joni Eareckson. *Joni: An Unforgettable Story*. With Joe Musser. Grand Rapids, MI: Zondervan Publishing House, 1976.

Thielicke, Helmut. *Being a Christian When the Chips Are Down.* Translated by H. George Anderson. Philadelphia: Fortress Press, 1979.

Thomas, Piri. *Down These Mean Streets.* New York: Vintage Books, 1974.

Thoreau, Henry David. *Walden* (1854), in *The Writings of Henry David Thoreau*, vol. 2, 155. Boston: Houghton Mifflin, 1906.

Weisel, Elie. *A Beggar in Jerusalem.* New York: Random House, 1970.

————. *The Town Beyond the Wall.* Translated from the French by Stephen Becker. New York: Holt, Rinehart and Winston, 1967.

White, Ed. *The Guideposts Treasury of Faith.* Garden City, NY: Doubleday, 1979.

Wumbrand, Richard. *In God's Underground.* New York: Bantam Books, 1977.

About the Author

When Mark Link, SJ, was a thirty-one-year-old Jesuit scholastic, he'd just begun writing the first of his more than sixty books, *Prayer for Millions*. He was pretty excited about the project, but one of his professors there, Fr. Edmund Fortman, SJ, wasn't as impressed. When Fr. Fortman heard he was trying to write a book, the professor asked, "What makes you think you have so much to say?"

Fr. Link, who will be eighty-five in April 2009, can't remember exactly how he answered, but he still remembers his excitement about writing. What excited him then, and continues to excite him, is discovering God's presence in the world: through prayer, in the news, in the stories he hears, in the lyrics of a song, or in the seemingly mundane occurrences that happen each and every day of each and every one of our lives.

As a young man, Fr. Link competed on a state tournament baseball team, earned the lead in two of his school plays, graduated, entered the Air Force, served for three years in the South Pacific theater, and earned three battle stars. When he returned, he put the GI Bill to work and enrolled in the architecture program at the University of Cincinnati. During his last three years of school, Fr. Link split time between classes at the University of Cincinnati and working for the city of Cleveland, where he did co-op work with the Austin Company, an architectural firm.

Watching the eldest son of the Cleveland family he lived with in the role of St. Edmund Campion, SJ, in a school play, Fr. Link was totally mesmerized. He began reading and inquiring about the Jesuits. He even began to picture himself as one.

Fr. Link's real clarity came later. At a benediction, there was a fifteen- to twenty-minute meditation during the exposition. That's when it really hit him: he was looking for something significant in his life. There was a hunger. Then it was clear: he should become a Jesuit. He just knew he should become a Jesuit.

Days later, he boarded a bus to return to Cincinnati for more classes. He slept for most of the ride. When he suddenly awoke, he saw outside the window, flashing past almost too fast for him to read, a sign: MILFORD 7 mi. Milford was the location of the Jesuit novitiate. After making a few retreats and designing a retreat house for his senior thesis, Fr. Link graduated in 1950, then entered the Milford novitiate the same year.

During his theology studies at West Baden College, he wrote a weekly column, "For Teens Only," for the Indianapolis archdiocesan newspaper.

He also began work on *Prayer for Millions*. By 1960, the year he was ordained for priestly ministry, he'd published his first book.

After he was ordained, he asked his provincial, Fr. John Connery, SJ, if he could enroll in a writing program at the University of South Carolina. "You don't need to go to writing school," Fr. Connery said. "You write just fine. You've just got to figure out something to say." The provincial sent him to Lumen Vitae, an institute in Brussels, Belgium, devoted to catechetics, where Fr. Link learned that he definitely had something to say.

In the forty-five years since, he's published more than sixty books, including *These Stones Will Shout*, *The Seventh Trumpet*, *Path through Scripture*, *Path through Catholicism*, *The New Catholic Vision*, and the 2000 Series that includes *Challenge*, *Vision*, *Mission*, *Action*, and *Psalms*. He also wrote a weekly column in *Faith Connections*, published by what is now RCL-Benziger. Along the way, Fr. Link scripted and was featured in twenty *Prayer and Scripture* video shows.

Fr. Link has given retreats in five English-speaking countries and lectured in nearly every major city in the United States. More than 700,000 of his books have been distributed in 800 prisons around the United States by the group Victory 2000.

During his prolific writing career, Fr. Link has also remained active as a teacher and pastor. He taught at

St. Ignatius College Prep in Chicago for seventeen years and spent three years on the Theology Staff at Loyola University. In the 1960s, he cofounded the Loyola Institute of Pastoral Studies and taught on its staff for eight summers. He taught seven years in the summer program of the National Institute for the Formation of the Clergy, and worked ten years in parish work in Plano, Texas.

In 2007, Fr. Link retired from teaching and moved to Loyola University, where he is a Writer-in-Residence. The current writing project that excites him most is a popular Web site called Stay Great (http://www.staygreat.com)—God made you great, so stay great. The site averages five thousand hits a day, has been accessed by users from 132 countries, and has regular visitors from over 60 countries. The site features two daily meditations (today and tomorrow) on the Mass reading of the day and contains five weekly features on Scripture, the Spiritual Exercises of St. Ignatius, and contemporary spirituality.

"As for writing," Fr. Link says, "it is just something I feel compelled to do. It's a great priestly ministry. You see things aren't the way you think they ought to be; and you want to change them. And there are so many stories out there. As Christians we've got one heck of a story to tell. That's what I'm trying to do."

Excerpted and updated from "Something to Say," G. R. Kearney, PARTNERS Magazine (Spring 2004): 16–20.